Further praise for *Attracting and Re...*

"While many books have identified
few have identified as clearly as 1
organizations to rethink their relationships between management
and employees. This important and accessible new book emphasizes
the need for new values and cultures to enable organizations
to innovate, adapt and renew their focus on customers, and it
provides clear, research-based and practical advice for managers and
employees to meet this need."

—Professor Peter Coaldrake, Vice-Chancellor,
QUT Graduate School of Business

"Tim Baker explains why organizations must change old ways and
shows how with the New Employment Relationship Model that
offers practical and powerful approaches to flexibility, collaboration,
customer focus, and performance orientation."

—Aubrey Warren, Pacific Training & Development

"A highly-recommended resource for business owners, human resource
practitioners, and managers. Tim Baker clearly articulates easy to
follow and innovative guidelines on becoming an employer of choice."

—Dr. Vicky Browning, MBA Director,
QUT Graduate School of Business

"The ideas and methods in Tim's book have been applied with
sensational results in several organizations I have been involved
with. Highly recommended reading."

—Dan McPherson, Executive Manager Organizational
Development and Engagement, Lockyer Valley Regional Council

"The suggestion of applying the research-based New Employment
Relationship Model, which identifies eight values of the new
psychological contract or employment relationship, is thought-
provoking."

—Commissioner Ian Stewart, Queensland Police Service

About the author

Dr Tim Baker is an international consultant and Managing Director of WINNERS-AT-WORK Pty Ltd (www.winnersatwork.com.au), which specializes in assisting managers to develop productive workplace cultures. Tim has conducted over 2,430 seminars, workshops, and keynote addresses to over 45,000 people in 11 countries across 21 industry groups over 18 years. He was voted one of the *50 Most Talented Global Training & Development Leaders* by the World HRD Congress. Tim is a successful author, executive coach, master trainer, visiting university lecturer, and keynote speaker.

Becoming an Employer of Choice

Attracting and Retaining Talent

Tim Baker

palgrave
macmillan

First published 2014 by
PALGRAVE MACMILLAN

Palgrave Macmillan in the UK is an imprint of Macmillan Publishers Limited, registered in England, company number 785998, of Houndmills, Basingstoke, Hampshire RG21 6XS.

Palgrave Macmillan in the US is a division of St Martin's Press LLC, 175 Fifth Avenue, New York, NY 10010.

Palgrave Macmillan is the global academic imprint of the above companies and has companies and representatives throughout the world.

Palgrave® and Macmillan® are registered trademarks in the United States, the United Kingdom, Europe and other countries.

ISBN 978–1–137–41173–0

This book is printed on paper suitable for recycling and made from fully managed and sustained forest sources. Logging, pulping and manufacturing processes are expected to conform to the environmental regulations of the country of origin.

A catalogue record for this book is available from the British Library.

A catalog record for this book is available from the Library of Congress.

Typeset by MPS Limited, Chennai, India.

I would like to dedicate this book to Carol, my wife and life partner for her enduring support, love, and kindness.

Contents

Introduction

Every organization these days wants to become an employer of choice. Many claim they are but, in reality, few can be considered as such. *Attracting and Retaining Talent* is concerned with how to become a genuine employer of choice. This means developing a workplace culture that reflects the changing needs and interests of both individual and organization.

In today's skills-short marketplace, many employers are adopting an employer of choice strategy, offering a variety of employee benefits in an attempt to attract and retain quality staff. A lot of these companies are doing this in a superficial way. It is often more about image than substance. The majority of today's employees are not influenced by employers' shallow claims of being an employer of choice. It is not as simple as offering prospective employees trinkets.

In plain terms, "employer of choice" means an organization that is a great place to work. If companies don't genuinely act to become an employer of choice then good employees will simply vote with their feet and move to a forward-thinking employer who offers them what they want. Being an employer of choice is more than marketing gimmickry.

"employer of choice" means an organization that is a great place to work.

Attracting and Retaining Talent is for anyone who is interested in fundamentally changing the culture of their organization. Finding and keeping top employees is critically important in the hyper-competitive workplace of the twenty-first century.

If enterprises cannot keep their best performers and at the same time recruit other stars to work with them, they are in trouble, or soon will be. More than anything else in the modern workplace, being a genuine employer of choice is the most tangible way to remain competitive in a climate of accelerated change and uncertainty.

For business owners, human resources (HR) practitioners and managers, *Attracting and Retaining Talent* offers a crystal-clear roadmap for developing a new, more productive workplace culture; one that is vastly different from the old mindset of the "them and us" employment relationship. This new culture is still based on an employee–employer relationship, but one founded on a working partnership that is poles apart from the conventional "them and us" approach; a more collaborative than adversarial relationship. This new kind of employment relationship reflects the changing needs of the modern employee and—at the same time—the interests of the progressive organization. This new way of relating is the cornerstone of being an employer of choice.

The centerpiece of *Attracting and Retaining Talent* is the New Employment Relationship Model. This model is research-based and identifies eight values of the new psychological contract or employment relationship. I suggest that, by applying this model in your workplace, you are creating the culture that underpins the employer of choice concept.

Chapter 1 defines the true essence of the overused term, "employer of choice." Being an employer of choice means being a workplace that aligns the changing needs and interests of individual and organization. I define the eight new values based on my research.

The needs of employees and employers have changed profoundly in a relatively short space of time. Chapter 2 explores those swiftly changing needs to provide readers with some clarity around the traditional employment relationship and juxtaposes this against the new employment relationship. I refer to this dynamic change in the employment relationship as the "workplace revolution."

One of the major impediments to developing a culture based on a new mindset about the employment relationship is the traditional way that people are developed within organizations. Approaches to human resource development (HRD) have generally failed to keep pace with the workplace revolution. Conventional responses to learning and development are no longer relevant in a fast-paced climate. A new way forward for HRD is way overdue. Chapter 3 looks at a new HRD paradigm.

Chapter 4 introduces the New Employment Relationship Model. The model takes into account the changing dynamics occurring from the beginnings of the workplace revolution discussed in the first three chapters. This revolution in the workplace greatly altered the expectations employees and employers have of each other. The model serves as a benchmark for organizations wanting to gauge their culture around the eight shared values outlined in Chapter 1.

In Chapter 5 we look at the application of the first of the eight values in the New Employment Relationship Model: flexible deployment. Flexible deployment is essentially about utilizing an employee's skills and abilities in a range of roles and work situations. It is increasingly the case that, for employees to work effectively and efficiently, they need to learn and apply a wider range of skills. Although flexible work practices are increasingly commonplace in the modern workplace, they are often not implemented properly, or for the right reasons. Done properly and for the right reasons, there are significant gains to be made for both the employee and the employer.

The second of the eight values in the model is customer focus. Over the past thirty or so years, the emphasis has shifted from a value of internal focus to a value of customer focus. We deal with this move in Chapter 6. Conventional thinking has suggested that, by having efficient processes and practices in place internally, organizations were likely to meet a reasonably clearly and consistently defined array of requests from their customer base. This internal focus on efficiency and consistency made good sense in a reasonably predictable marketplace. Now, with an increasingly unpredictable marketplace, a new way is needed. This new approach means those employees who deal directly with customers must be problem solvers who go beyond simple adherence to an organization's policies and processes. They now have to juggle the often competing needs of the company and the customer.

The third value is performance focus, discussed in Chapter 7. Despite all the attention paid to performance in the management literature, most performance management systems are inadequate. These systems—more often than not—ignore dimensions of work performance that are not specifically job-related. I am strongly advocating a broader interpretation of performance that goes beyond job-specific behaviors. This new definition of performance promises to support and reinforce desirable workplace accomplishment.

The traditional hierarchically structured organization has served us well for two hundred years. But the functionally-based organizational structure is generally pretty inflexible and slow to change direction. It is unsuitable for the twenty-first century. Organizations structured around divisions, departments, units, branches, or sections are less responsive to fluctuations in market conditions. The nature of work today is more project-based than functional. Most issues need quick input from several sources within an organizational structure. The value of project-based work is the focus of Chapter 8.

From an employee's perspective, work increasingly defines their self-concept and connection to others. And, yet, accelerated change and uncertainty in the workplace are turning work from something that was once considered stable and predictable into a source of profound insecurity. People are now changing jobs more frequently and the workforce is becoming increasingly fragmented. So, on the one hand, people want more meaning from their work for a variety of reasons. But, on the other hand, employees are being told there is "no long term." These are confusing signals. Chapter 9 tackles the value of human spirit and work.

Yet another binding value of the New Employment Relationship Model is commitment. In the traditional employee–employer relationship, an underpinning value was loyalty. In a traditional employment relationship, employees would display loyalty to the organization and, in exchange, they would receive loyalty from the organization in terms of a clearly defined career path and opportunities to build a career. What employers now need is a committed employee who assists them to achieve the goals of the business. Younger employees in particular also would rather have a committed employer than a loyal one. It is for this reason that commitment has replaced loyalty as a mutual exchange process between employer and employee, and this value is discussed in Chapter 10.

The value of learning and development takes a multidimensional approach to HRD. Training, on the other hand, is one-dimensional and based essentially on the production-centered approach. Missing in traditional HRD programs is the person-centered and problem-solving approaches. We discuss this in Chapter 11.

Chapter 12 considers the line between employee initiative and managerial responsibility, referred to as the initiative paradox. The initiative paradox is defined as managing the extent and limits of employee participation in decision-making. It is therefore tied to the flow and quality of information that provides a responsive environment to enable appropriate participation by employees in organizational decision-making. Open information is the eighth and final value in the model.

Finally, Chapter 13 introduces readers to the corporate culture change cycle, a methodology for creating a culture reflective of the New Employment Relationship Model. I use a case study to illustrate the way it is implemented in the workplace.

Enjoy!

The Eight Changing Values

Businesses that don't embrace and promote these new values are likely to become less and less appealing places to work for good employees who value this new way of thinking.

I vividly recall training a group of professionals on the virtues of completing the ubiquitous "to-do list" many years ago. Sound familiar?

As I passionately proclaimed the merits of doing this simple but powerful task to my audience, I noticed their eyes becoming glazed. They were tuning out instead of tuning in.

I could see clearly from this that these leaders weren't going to take my well-intentioned advice and make a to-do list.

Why? Why wouldn't you do something so simple and effective? I thought.

Then it dawned on me … The power of what goes on outside the four walls of the training room has more influence than I or any other trainer could ever muster.

The workplace to which these leaders belonged had a "fly by the seat of your pants" culture. In other words, they weren't convinced that being organized would work in their current organizational culture. It made me think, if I could change the culture of the workplace, I could change these leaders' mindsets about a simple organizing tool like the to-do list and many other things.

I truly understood for the first time that sustainable change is about changing people's thinking. But, if I could change people's thinking, I could change their behavior.

If you are an employer or manager, imagine for a moment if you had a million prospective employees knocking at your door looking for a job every single year. Surveys show that most people dread going to work every day. Imagine for a moment what it would be like to work in an organization that is often more fun than being at home with your family. Are these two situations a pipe dream? No, it's not a dream, it's reality. Google, the iconic Californian-based search engine giant, is such a workplace. Consistently voted one of the best places to work in corporate America, Google receives 3,000 applications a day—which equates to one million applications a year—from people wanting a job. They are all chasing about 4,000 jobs. Employees who are lucky enough to work at Google claim that they often have more fun at work than at home. Yet Google is posting record profits. These remarkable features are no accident. Eric Schmidt, Google's executive chairman, believes that Google's competitive advantage in the marketplace is not superior products and services: it is their workplace culture. Google is an employer of choice.

Attracting and Retaining Talent is for anyone who is interested in fundamentally changing the culture of their organization. It does not matter whether you are working in a public or private-sector organization, or a small, medium-sized or large enterprise. If you cannot keep your best performers and at the same time recruit other stars to work with you, you are in trouble, or soon will be. In the modern workplace, this is the most tangible way to be—and remain—competitive in a climate of accelerated change and uncertainty.

What is an employer of choice?

In plain terms, employer of choice means an organization that is a great place to work. If companies don't genuinely act to become an employer of choice, then good employees will simply vote with their feet and move to a forward-thinking employer that offers them what they want. Being an employer of choice is more than a marketing gimmick.

An employer of choice is a flexible, customer-focused, performance-oriented organization, one that is more maneuverable and engages the hearts and minds of their people. This kind of workplace culture is characterized by great commitment from employees to achieve the organization's vision. An employer of choice is continuously learning, developing, and improving. Employees are relentlessly encouraged to be enterprising and resourceful, and they respond to this challenge willingly and consistently.

The opposite characteristics can be observed in the traditional organization, based on the "them and us" mindset. These places of work are rigid and inflexible, are more focused on themselves than the customer, lack exceptional performance, are set in their ways and practices; workers leave their brains "in a paper bag at the door" when they come to work. Instead of learning from their mistakes, employees cover up their mistakes: they stop learning. Employees are directed to follow systems and processes and taught not to question the way things are done. Unfortunately, there are still many organizations operating like this today.

From my research and observations in over a decade as an international consultant, I believe it boils down to the nature of the relationship between the boss and the worker. The "them and us" mentality is perpetuated by habit and tradition, some militant trade unions, and managers and employees who think this is the way it ought to be. Yet it is the backdrop for an inflexible and rigid workplace: one that has poor customer relations and that is more concerned about the start and finish time of workers each day than focusing on their real performance. Employees are disengaged and find their work meaningless. Companies of this ilk will not hesitate to reward a mediocre employee with a widescreen plasma TV for twenty years' of service, but will chastise an energetic employee for showing initiative. Managers will sponsor training, but only if it directly affects the bottom line: personal development is non-existent and viewed as a waste of money. People who mindlessly follow systems are favored over others who want to do things their way. It is therefore not surprising that most people don't want to work in this sort of place. This type of culture is entirely unsuitable for meeting the challenges of the modern marketplace. An organization with this traditional approach to the employment relationship is an employer of choice too. But the difference is that people actively make a choice *not* to work there—and those who do, do not have a choice. I recently read a great saying that sums up this predicament: the only rats that leave a sinking ship are the ones that can swim!

What does an employer of choice have to offer employees?

Employees are attracted to employers of choice for a variety of reasons. People are encouraged and supported to grow on the job, and develop a broader array of capabilities. For example, people are often given the opportunity to master a variety of skills, and this gives them more scope to apply for other jobs in other enterprises. But, ironically, they often choose to stay because of the attraction of this wide-ranging approach to developing people's capacities. An employer of choice will most likely have good support structures in place for dealing with customers. These superior systems reduce stress and focus employees on their primary task: to provide effective solutions for customers. Employees are rewarded and recognized for high performance. Many organizational members respond well to these incentives and consequently lift their performance. Cross-functional communication is encouraged. Departments and divisions are not as important in these adaptable structures. Most people are fully engaged in their work and committed to achieving the goals of the enterprise. They are encouraged to think and act freely and not be constrained and dependent on the organization. Employees are well informed and have complete access to all the information they need for do their work. These benefits are appreciated by employees and attractive to prospective employees.

How many progressively-minded employees want to be locked into jobs with a restricted range of skills, mindlessly following internal systems and processes that fail to consistently address the immediate needs of the end user? Good employees want to be recognized and rewarded for exceptional performance rather than receiving pay parity, regardless of how they perform their work. They are not likely to want to work in a departmental structure with a silo mentality that separates them from the rest of the organization. Modern employees are generally happy to commit to achieving business goals, but don't necessarily want to be subservient to a boss. People with the right attitude want to grow and develop from their work but not necessarily be dependent on the organization. It is natural for people to want to know what is going on and not be told on a "need to know" basis. Employees are quite capable and ready to express initiative in the right circumstances with the right information and encouragement. This old employment relationship mindset is increasingly less attractive to capable workers.

The roadmap to become an employer of choice is based on a new mindset supported by eight values. Collectively, these eight shared values are what I refer to as the New Employment Relationship

Model. This set of values forms the basis for a new working relationship that is diametrically opposite to the old employment relationship. Each value of the new mindset is the reverse of the eight values that have defined the "them and us" relationship we have observed since the birth of industry. Although this traditional employment mindset has been unraveling for some time, old ways of thinking are still entrenched in the workplace.

What is the traditional employment mindset?

The traditional relationship between employee and employer has been in existence for over two hundred years since the Industrial Revolution. But this conventional relationship is under considerable strain. As the world of work evolves, employees and employers are increasingly unsure of what their role is in the relationship. This uncertainty is creating a lot of tension in contemporary workplaces that extends across all industries.

For example, employees with a traditional mindset about their role expect their boss to tell them what to do. Assuming, of course, that it is not an unreasonable demand, the traditional-thinking employee sees their role as one of complying with the boss's requests. These employees find it hard to cope with a forward-thinking manager who expects them to think for themselves. In reverse, traditional-thinking managers expect employees to follow directions and not question their wisdom. They do not cope well with employees who show initiative and enterprise. So, enterprising employees will undoubtedly be frustrated by an autocratic boss. These situations of role confusion are commonplace and create anxiety and misunderstanding in today's workplaces. But fifty years ago, employees and employers were clear about their roles. For instance, a manager who invites employees to think for themselves would be branded weak and indecisive, and an employee who showed initiative may well be considered by their boss to be a troublemaker. The roles were clear-cut and respected.

But now, more than ever, employees want and expect to think for themselves without always deferring to their boss. Similarly, an employer of choice wants and expects employees to be flexible, customer-oriented, focused on performance, engaged, committed, dedicated to their own growth and development, and to exercise appropriate initiative. This type of culture is likely to be threatening to an employee or manager with a twentieth-century mindset about their role in the employment relationship. This evolving relationship is now less clear-cut and may therefore create widespread confusion and frustration for managers and employees in the twenty-first century.

Under the traditional "them and us" relationship, it was expected that employees work hard, cause few problems, and generally do whatever the boss wants. In return, it was expected that employers would provide "good jobs" with good pay, offer plenty of advancement opportunities, and virtually guarantee lifetime employment. In this relatively stable and predictable world, the employee would be loyal to the employer and in return the employer would provide job security for the employee. This unwritten agreement between the two parties came to be referred to as the psychological contract.

Since the 1980s, the relatively secure and predictable marketplace has been replaced by rapid change, uncertainty, and global competition. The consequence of this swiftly evolving global economy has placed considerable pressure and tension on this old working relationship. It has called into question employees' and employers' preconceptions of their working relationship. Changes in the marketplace since the latter part of the twentieth century have altered forever the requirements of organizations and employees. As a consequence, expectations of what managers and employees should do and not do are entirely different to what they were. I refer to this rapidly changing psychological contract as the workplace revolution in my previous book, *The 8 Values of Highly Productive Companies: Creating Wealth from a New Employment Relationship.*[1]

Why is there widespread confusion and frustration today?

As a result of this lack of role clarity, employees and employers now send and receive confusing signals from each other. Employees are increasingly unsure about what organizational leaders want or expect from them. Do managers want me to be a Jack or Jill of all trades or a specialist? Do managers want me to be customer-focused or to follow strict organizational policies and procedures? Do they want me to follow my job description to the letter, or do they want me to do whatever needs to be done to get the work done? Management wants me to be engaged in my work, but I'm disengaged. What do I do? Am I supposed to be loyal or committed to the company, or both? Am I supposed to develop myself technically or personally, or both? Does my manager want me to show initiative, or do I follow the system? And so on. Employees are currently faced with these dilemmas daily.

At this time, managers are equally confused. Should I be giving employees specifically defined work tasks to do, or help them to become multi-skilled? Do I want my staff to show initiative when dealing with customers, or should they follow standard operating procedures for consistency of service? Are job descriptions worth the paper they are written on? How do I break down this silo mentality and promote communication between departments? How do I engage my people in their work? How do I find and keep good employees? Am I wasting money developing employees—won't

---

[1] Baker, T.B. (2009) *The 8 Values of Highly Productive Companies: Creating Wealth from a New Employment Relationship*. Brisbane: Australian Academic Press.

they just walk out the door and use their training with our competitors? How do I get my employees to show initiative when I need them to, and how do I curb their initiative at other times? These are some of the daily predicaments facing managers.

We are in a state of flux between two opposing mindsets. The current uncertainty about people's organizational roles and responsibilities is because we haven't yet made a complete transition from the old to the new. We are familiar with the roles and responsibilities of the old employment relationship, which is straightforward but unsuitable for the present. We are making tentative moves towards a new working relationship. Although it is being extensively discussed, there is no clarity around what employee and employer should give and receive in this new psychological contract.

What does this new relationship look like, and what does it offer individuals and organizations? This is the central question I attempt to answer in *Attracting and Retaining Talent*. A new working relationship is the launching pad to becoming an employer of choice. This new mindset is good for business and at the same time addresses the needs of the modern employee. Like bees to honey, an employer of choice will attract the right employees and retain current ones.

If you are an employee coming up to retirement, you will have first-hand experience of the conventional "them and us" employment relationship. More experienced employees will also appreciate that the traditional relationship is under pressure. In the same way, more mature managers will notice that younger workers have an entirely different outlook about their role: their expectations are poles apart from those of older employees. In these kinds of situations there is inevitably a clash of values.

We all know instinctively that the employment relationship is evolving. Despite knowing this, we have no clear guide to assist us through this unfamiliar terrain. The odd seminar on how to handle Generation X or Generation Y is of little value. They can reinforce stereotypes. For instance, baby boomers who criticize younger staff for not being loyal won't work, and employees crying out for more freedom and autonomy are likely to fall on deaf ears in traditionally-run companies. The majority of books on organizational development do not give a clear description of what this radically new landscape looks like and how to deal with it.

The evolution of the employment relationship has affected the culture of the modern workplace. Workplace culture is really about the way we do things around here. All businesses, whether large or small, have a unique culture. Workplace culture can be created by accident or design. More than any other factor, the culture within an organization is the result of the relationship between managers and employees.

What does the New Employment Relationship Model offer?

The New Employment Relationship Model offers people in the workforce, or starting out in employment, ways of integrating successfully in the forward-thinking workplace. It provides a path of certainty: a way forward. With a fresh understanding, employees— irrespective of how long they have been with a company—can shape their careers in a way that matches this new paradigm. Employees who respond to this changing employment relationship will reap the rewards of a prosperous working life.

I will address several important questions about this new mindset throughout the book:

- How has the employment relationship—the foundation of industry—changed over the past thirty years, and how will this affect current and future organizational leaders and members?
- What are the eight shared values that support the radically changing employment relationship, and how are these values different from the old employment relationship?

- How do these changing values influence the way people should be managed and led in the workplace? And how do these principles shape employees and their careers?
- What do managers need to do differently to lead in this new reality? And what is the best way for employees to boost their career prospects?
- How can we successfully benchmark these new values in organizations?

You may be thinking, I've heard all this before. How is *Attracting and Retaining Talent* different from the plethora of management and leadership books on the bookshelves around the world?

Attracting and Retaining Talent is unlike other books because it looks at the development of the individual and organization from an entirely different perspective. In essence, the New Employment Relationship Model examines the role employers and employees need to play in the context of the shifting psychological contract. This is done by laying out a specific pathway to becoming a true employer of choice. It is based on a series of clearly defined benchmarks rather than generalizing about the new world of work. This roadmap is concerned with modeling the changing requirements of employee and employer, and how both entities should think and act in their own best interests and the interests of the other party. Essentially, I am offering a fresh agreement that benefits both partners in the enduring employment relationship. This provides a certainty that has been missing in the contemporary workplace.

What are the eight shared values of an employer of choice?

Table 1.1 illustrates the changing values of the psychological contract.

Table 1.1   The changing values of the psychological contract

Traditional values	New values
Specialized employment	Flexible deployment
Internal focus	Customer focus
Job focus	Performance focus
Functional-based work	Project-based work
Human dispirit and work	Human spirit and work
Loyalty	Commitment
Training	Learning and development
Closed information	Open information

You will notice that the eight new values on the right-hand side are diametrically opposite to the traditional values supporting the traditional employment relationship on the left-hand side. Managers who want their organizations to become an employer of choice ought to be instilling the eight principles on the right-hand side. These eight values form the framework for being an employer of choice. They are shared values between the employees and management. The shared values of flexible deployment, customer focus, performance focus, project-based work, human spirit and work, commitment, learning and development, and open information are consistent with the changing requirements of organizations and individuals.

Briefly, the eight values are defined as follows:

- *Flexible deployment* is the provision of a functionally flexible workforce. This means that employees are multi-skilled wherever possible. A multi-skilled workforce translates into a flexible and maneuverable business in a rapidly changing marketplace.
- *Customer focus* means removing internal organizational obstacles to focus on the requirements of the customer. Everything that is thought of, said, or done in a company ought to be done with the customer in mind.

- *Performance focus* links rewards and benefits with performance rather than organizational dependency. "A fair day's work for a fair day's pay" is a mindset that is no longer relevant and is counter to developing a focus on performance.
- *Project-based work* means organizing work around projects rather than organizational functions. Project-based work encourages cross-functional communication and breaks down internal barriers.
- *Human spirit and work* is connecting the work that employees do with personal meaning. Finding meaning in work engages employees and contributes to greater productivity and lower staff turnover.
- *Learning and development* means shifting from a focus on a training culture to a broader emphasis on learning and development. A learning and development culture means that employees are continually learning and growing on the job, both professionally and personally.
- *Commitment* to and from employees is a more practical substitute for the outdated idea of organizational loyalty. A business that is committed to assisting employees to grow and develop and manage their work–life responsibilities is more likely to gain commitment from its employees to achieve business goals.
- *Open information* means communicating the necessary information about the company and its direction to employees so that they can understand and appreciate the business decisions that are made. Moving from a closed to an open information culture aligns the perspective of employees with the organization.

I explain these shared eight values from the dual perspective of organization and individual in more depth in subsequent chapters.

Businesses that do not embrace these new values are likely to become less and less appealing places to work for good employees, who are likely to believe in this new mindset and share its values.

Companies holding on to the old mindset supported by a different set of values will struggle to keep and attract top talent.

The old way of thinking illustrated by the set of values on the left-hand side of the table has been slow to change, and there are various pressures to hold on to this paradigm. As mentioned earlier, this time-honored mindset has been a very successful factor in the growth of industry since the dawn of the Industrial Revolution. This psychological contract has not come under scrutiny until the last few decades. What is more, the impressive expansion of the marketplace over a long period has deeply entrenched the virtues of the conventional "them and us" employment relationship in our psyche. There is strong pressure from interest groups such as old guard trade unions, traditionally-minded employer associations and both left-wing and right-wing political parties to prolong the struggle for their own gain. Furthermore, because of the simplicity and durability of the traditional psychological contract, it is very difficult for employees and employers to let go of their dependency on the old conventions. After all, if it has worked for at least two centuries, why change it? These incentives to hold on to the conventional employment relationship make it tough to change the culture of an organization.

Is the challenge worth it?

Challenging as it surely is, it is timely for people to revisit their thinking about the employment relationship. This means employees and organizational leaders questioning the relevance and effectiveness of the old mindset against the backdrop of a dramatically altered marketplace characterized by accelerated change and uncertainty. Without taking into account the shifting psychological contract, managers will continue to cobble together a series of unsustainable growth strategies. Outdated approaches to bring out the best in employees will continue to fail. What is required is a completely different view of how organizational leaders and employees relate to each other.

And without understanding the changing relationship, employees are likely to continue to be baffled about their work contribution and asphyxiate their careers. Employees will benefit from a fresh view of what they can offer organizations. Traditionally, employees have been eager to specialize and have seen no need to broaden their skills set; willing to measure their success by complying with company processes over pleasing the customer; honor their working hours over performance on the job; demonstrate allegiance to their department over the wider organization; do work because they have to, not because they want to; exhibit dependence on the organization over independence; achieve qualifications over lifelong learning; and be compliant over displaying initiative. Although there is evidence that attitudes are changing, employees will do themselves, their career, and the organizations they are employed by more good if they think differently about their work and what they have to offer in a changing global economy.

Confidence comes from certainty and certainty comes from the right information. There are many strategies for managing people and getting the best from them. But unfortunately these approaches do not openly explain how employees' requirements are shifting and how these needs affect the employment relationship. This strategic advice is mostly employer-centric and neglects the employee's role. There is, to date, very little practical advice on managing the employment relationship. I am interested in filling this void. To be an effective HR practitioner, organizational leader, or enterprising employee, you would do well to heed this information about why the new psychological contract is emerging and what you can do to accommodate this evolution.

HR professionals are called on more and more to create productive workplace cultures, at least at the strategic level. Having a clear roadmap can only assist in this regard. As you will read in Chapter 3, the HRD profession—in my view—is at a crossroads. The profession needs to change its thinking and approach or risk irrelevancy. Having a methodical approach to changing an organization's culture can therefore only be an asset.

If you are an employee—and we have all been at some stage of our career—you will gain a better insight into how the psychological contract is evolving and how best to respond to improve your career prospects. Qualities like job security, qualifications, certainty, and organizational dependence were once critical to your career success; but no more. The traits for success are now employability, commitment to continuous improvement, flexibility, and independence: the paradoxical characteristics for a successful employee in the twentieth century. Understanding why and how this new mindset can be applied is likely to enhance an employee's career in a global and dynamic marketplace. This information answers the question: what attitudes and qualities does an employer of choice look for in an employee?

For managers, concepts such as paternalism, having ownership of employees' development, offering clearly defined career paths, having secretive plans for top employees, minimizing the information flow on a "need to know" basis, and rewarding only vertical progression in organizations are now obsolete. These ideas are being replaced by empowering and enabling people, being prepared to partner employees in their growth and development, recognizing and promoting multiple ways for staff to move on and progress, accepting that employees are now ultimately responsible for their own careers, opening up the channels of communication, and linking compensation to contribution. These are some of the attitudes and qualities needed for managerial success. Again—as for employees— these features are diametrically opposite to the traditional employers' response. This fresh approach to organizational leadership will be attractive to the growing number of employees who are embracing the new mindset.

These features are not shallow observations. The eight value shifts illustrated in Table 1.1 have been thoroughly investigated and researched in organizational settings across industry groups, countries, and public- and private-sector organizations. I have used examples and anecdotes from some of the world's best companies to show how they are coping with these changes successfully. This provides some context and practical illustrations of what you can do in your own organization to better reflect this emerging relationship between employee and employer.

To begin this journey, Chapter 2 looks at the changing world of work and some of the global and economic pressures that have transformed the psychological contract. Earlier in this chapter, I referred to this transformation as the workplace revolution. This workplace revolution is largely responsible for profoundly altering, forever, the psychological contract between employee and employer.

The **10** Key Points …

1. *Attracting and Retaining Talent* offers you a roadmap for developing a new, more productive workplace culture, one that is vastly different from the traditional mindset of the "them and us" employment relationship.

2. An employer of choice is an organization that is a great place to work.

3. The traditional "them and us" employment relationship has been around since the beginning of the Industrial Revolution and, while there is lots of pressure to hold on to this psychological contract, there is also increasing pressure to change it.

④ An employer of choice offers employees an expanded skills set, support to build better customer relationships, rewards for high performance, better access to stakeholders across the organization, meaningful work, commitment to aid careers through holistic learning opportunities, and open information channels.

⑤ An employer of choice is flexible and maneuverable, customer-focused, performance-focused, project-based rather than silo-based, filled with people who find meaning in their work and are committed to achieving success, and has a highly skilled and adaptive workforce who are prepared to use their initiative.

⑥ There is widespread confusion and frustration in organizations today because employees and employers are uncertain about their roles and responsibilities: the psychological contract is in flux between the old and new.

⑦ The values of the traditional employment relationship are specialized employment, internal focus, job focus, functional-based work, human dispirit and work, loyalty, training, and closed information.

⑧ The values of the new employment relationship are flexible deployment, customer focus, performance focus, project-based work, human spirit and work, commitment, learning and development, and open information.

⑨ Although challenging, it is timely for people to overhaul their thinking about the employment relationship.

⑩ The roadmap provides employees and managers with a degree of certainty about the way forward.

The New World of Work

Organizations that will thrive in this new reality are those that are filled with employees who have the option to leave, but choose to stay because of the work.

Hasbro is an employee-friendly place to work. Almost every one of its 3,055 employees gets paid to do volunteer work for children for four hours a month. There's a company store with big discounts on merchandise and, in return for an extra four hours of work between Monday and Thursday, everyone apart from shift workers gets Friday afternoons off. These two much-loved policies—which cost the company relatively little—earn enormous goodwill from the workforce. So does the Edy's frozen-yogurt machine in the cafeteria, requisitioned by the CEO.

But the chief reason that employees enjoy working at Hasbro is that it's fun. Every new employee gets a Mr. or Mrs. Potato Head. You can imagine the employees who work at this leading toy-maker are very popular with their children!

If Hasbro's games plant in Western Massachusetts is a vestige of American manufacturing power, its corporate headquarters in blue-collar Pawtucket, Rhode Island, reflect the reinvention of a mighty $4 billion international brand. The combination of old and new is central to Hasbro's culture. Not *that long ago, Hasbro's core properties—toys like G.I. Joe and Transformers, as well as games like Battleship—were languishing; a company founded in 1923 was too focused on licenses such as Pokémon and Batman. It was accepted wisdom that the toys and games business was subject to fads, and products had a natural life cycle, including oblivion. What Hasbro saw was a strategic opportunity to exploit its brands across a range of media, not just new platforms such as iPads, but on TV and in film. As Brian Goldner, CEO, put it: "We have a vault of 1,500 assets. We are not just in the toy and game business—we're in the intellectual property and entertainment business." Hasbro now has its own film office and TV studio in Los Angeles.[1]*

Imagine for a moment how you would feel if you had devoted more than thirty years of loyal service to a company, working hard and climbing the corporate ladder to a "secure" middle management position, only to be told suddenly that your services were no longer needed by that company. You pack your bags and walk out the door for the last time. On the drive home, you think to yourself: How will I break this to my wife? You were promised a job for life. You have just bought your first investment property and start to panic.

If this hasn't happened to you, you probably know someone who has experienced this: it may be your father, or a close friend. You would, no doubt, feel bitterness and a sense of betrayal. Others who have kept their job in the company would have mixed feelings. They would be relieved that they didn't have a target on their backs. They would also undoubtedly feel sorry for that person and probably think it was unfair and harsh. At any rate, the situation wouldn't be pleasant for anyone, including the person doing the firing.

This scenario was precisely what happened to lots of people in the mid to late 1980s. The workplace revolution was underway. Its genesis was massive layoffs across all industries. This was particularly

---

[1] Kaplin, D.A. (2011) "Undercover employee: A day on the job at three best companies." *Fortune*, p. 41.

severe in large corporate enterprises. The majority of these sackings occurred to layers of middle managers. This wholesale clear-out led to a violation of trust between employee and employer. Employees who had in many cases given decades of service to companies were thrown on the scrap heap. Naturally, employees lost faith in the time-honored employment relationship. Employers were keen to cut costs and the "overhead" of labor was where savings could be made. The result was that a stratum of mid-level employees was ripped out of the organizational structure across most industry groups. This state of affairs was the beginning of the end for the traditional employment relationship as we have come to know it. Globalization then accelerated the movement away from the values of the traditional employment relationship (discussed in Chapter 1).

What is the workplace revolution?

The "them and us" employment relationship is a relic of the past century. As I mentioned in Chapter 1, many organizations still exhibit characteristics of this traditional working relationship. Some have made the transformation and become genuine employers of choice; sadly, these are few and far between. I have illustrated some of these forward-thinking companies throughout the book. The marketplace is increasingly volatile and unpredictable. In response, companies have to be nimble, customer-centric, with flatter structures. They require engaged and committed workers, in a culture that promotes innovation, learning, enterprise, and open communication. That cannot be achieved with a shared "them and us" mentality. A different approach is needed to handle the relatively tumultuous environment of the early twenty-first century.

In contrast to the twenty-first century, the twentieth century was a relatively stable and predictable marketplace. Apart from a few exceptions, it enjoyed a steady commercial environment. The

Great Depression of 1929 and the stock market crash of 1987 are two episodes that come to mind that were the exception rather than the rule. But in this steady, conventional marketplace, the old employment conventions functioned exceptionally well. Now, this long-established employment relationship—the one that most of us have experienced first-hand in our working lives—is now causing more harm than good.

Globalization—and the heightened competition this invites from all corners of the planet—has challenged companies to be more responsive to the many and varied fluctuations in market conditions and trends. To survive and remain competitive, organizational leaders have applied a multitude of strategies without much sustainable success. Many of these conventional approaches have only tinkered at the edges of transforming organizations. They have failed to get to the heart of the matter—which is the inadequacies of the old employee–employer relationship.

How have the needs of employees changed?

As the needs of enterprises have changed, the new economy has fundamentally changed the needs of workers too. For instance, a successful career in the twentieth century was based on three pillars: a secure job, often with the same company for an employee's entire career, qualifications, and demonstrated loyalty to the employer. These needs have now been turned upside down. A successful career in the twenty-first century is based on employability, continuous learning, and independence.

A successful career in the twenty-first century is based on employability, continuous learning, and independence.

Table 2.1 illustrates the changing needs of employees from the past century to this century.

Table 2.1   The changing needs of employees

Twentieth century	Twenty-first century
Job security	Employability
Technical capacity	Communication capacity
Jobs	Roles
Functional work	Cross-functional work
Careers	Meaningful work
Long-term loyalty	Short-term commitment
Qualifications	Lifelong learning
Reliability	Enterprise

Forward-thinking employees—ones that organizations need to attract and retain—want to work in places where their needs are met; these are shown in the right-hand column. Today, employees want to maintain and build their employability rather than rely on a secure job. They understand that the concept of job security is a thing of the past. Having a portfolio of skills and capabilities that are attractive and adaptable in a variety of employment situations is a more practical consideration. They appreciate that technical competence is now a commodity that can easily be duplicated or replaced. The ability to communicate effectively with customers and colleagues gives them a distinctive value-added competitive advantage. Rather than a clearly defined job description, modern employees understand that their work role is broader than the confines of a job statement of duties. Being innovative, functioning effectively in a team, and continually learning and growing are additional roles beyond their job role: they all benefit their employment. Working in multidisciplinary teams on short- and long-term projects is recognized by them to be more important than working in a silo with allegiance to a departmental head. Increasingly, people are more interested in doing work that they find meaningful rather than faithfully following a long-term career path. The average employee of the twenty-first century is spending less and less time working in one organization. They prefer to demonstrate short-term commitment toward the purpose of the organization rather than exercising long-term dependency and loyalty. Modern employees understand that they cannot stand still: they must keep learning and growing. Formal qualifications are only the starting point in their development. Of course, not all employees understand and seek out these things. But the ones who do are on the lookout for employers who demonstrate those values.

The challenges for employees in the twenty-first century are vastly different from those of the twentieth century. In the twentieth century the test was: How do I find a secure job? Now in the twenty-first century they are challenged with: How do I maintain my currency and employability? In the past century, the challenge was: What internal systems and processes do I need to follow to ensure a good outcome to the customer? This has been replaced by a focus on the issue of: How do I build a long-term relationship with a customer? In the twentieth century, the question was: How do I find a clearly defined job that I can be measured against? Now the challenge is: How do I find a job in an organization that gives me the scope to develop and grow? In the twentieth century, the challenge was: How do I learn to function in a departmental regime? Now the challenge is: How do I learn to function with many and varied stakeholders? In the twentieth century, the challenge was: How do I build a career? Now it is more likely to be: How do I find meaningful work? In the twentieth century, the challenge was: How do I find an organization that will show me a sense of loyalty? The twenty-first century challenge is: How do I find an organization that is willing to commit to assisting me in achieving my goals? In the twentieth century, the challenge was: How do I get the necessary technical qualifications to compete for good jobs? Now the challenge is: How do I continually grow and develop to maintain my employability? The twentieth-century challenge was: How do I display to my employer a sense of reliability? Now the challenge is more likely to be: How do I display to my employer a sense of initiative?

The new century raises new questions and many challenges for employees.

How have the needs of organizations changed?

Just as the needs of employees have profoundly changed in the workplace revolution, so too have the needs of employers (Table 2.2).

The ever-changing and hyper-competitive marketplace we now live and work in requires companies to be flexible. Being stable and predictable was important in the relatively steady economic conditions of the past century. Everything a company does now needs to take account of the customer: consumers have more options than ever before and, if unsatisfied, are quite prepared to exercise their options. Moreover, the wisdom of the past century was quality assurance: that is, by having quality systems and processes in place, organizations could minimize the margins for error in servicing their customers. The job description was the building block of the twentieth-century organization, attempting

Table 2.2   The changing needs of employers

Twentieth century	Twenty-first century
Stability	Maneuverability
Quality assurance	Customer responsiveness
Clearly defined jobs	Clearly defined performance indicators
Hierarchy	Malleability
Career paths	Engagement
Loyal workforce	Committed workforce
Qualified staff	Learning organization
Compliance	Initiative

to spell out the employee's tasks and responsibilities. Now the focus is on spelling out key performance criteria. The structure of the twentieth-century organization was typically hierarchical and was illustrated as such in an organizational chart. In contrast, work structured around projects is now a more superior organizing model than hierarchy. Work is more likely to cross functional boundaries and be fragmented; the traditional organization chart doesn't easily reflect this reality. Climbing the corporate ladder was an inducement for the ambitious employee of the twentieth century. Now the "ladder" is likely to be a lot shorter in most organizations and leaning up against a wall that may not be very steady. Now, an employee who is completely engaged in their field of work is a more attractive proposition to an organization than a ladder climber. Having a committed and loyal employee is an asset for a company. But if a company had to choose between the two values, commitment would win out. An organization where employees are constantly growing and developing and sharing their knowledge is what the modern employer wants. Formal qualifications are now only considered by organizational leaders as a starting point. An employee who is enterprising is now more valued than one who simply demonstrates compliance. Like employees, not all employers exhibit these twenty-first-century traits.

The key challenges for the twenty-first-century organization are markedly different to those of the past century. These issues today include: How can we flexibly deploy and develop the skill sets of our staff so that we are more maneuverable? Whereas the challenge of the twentieth century was: How can we find employees with specialized skill sets? In the twentieth century the challenge was to create an internally focused set of systems and processes to provide consistency in terms of dealing with the customer. Now the challenge is: How do we create an organization where everything that is said and done is focused on the customer? The twentieth-century test was: How do we create clearly defined and structured jobs that make the employee easy to manage? Now the question is: How do we get employees to focus on performance rather than merely doing their job? In the twentieth century the challenge was: How can we provide our employees with a clearly defined and attractive career path? Now it is: How do we capture the hearts and minds of employees? The old challenge was: How do we find employees who will be loyal to our company? Today's challenge is: How do we find employees who will be committed to our vision? The old challenge was: How do we find qualified staff who are technically proficient to do their job? Now the challenge is: How do we provide an environment where employees can grow on the job? The twentieth-century challenge was: How do we use information channels to prescribe strict processes and procedures? Now the challenge is: How do we use information channels to encourage employees to show appropriate initiative? Just as it does for employees, the new century raises new questions for employers.

From the contemporary requirements of the employee and employer illustrated in the right-hand column of Tables 2.1 and 2.2, the key is to align these two sets of needs in a new psychological contract. In other words, by bringing into line the modern requirements of individual and organization, this forms the basis of a new employment relationship. This is essentially what employers of choice do: they give employees what they need and merge these requirements with their own enterprise needs. This alliance creates a culture that is both appealing to forward-thinking employees and adaptive to market forces. Individuals who still harbor the old values shown in the left-hand column of the table are unlikely to find an employer of choice a desirable place to work, and will probably be more comfortable working in organizations with a traditional culture. Then again, an employer of choice is not likely to be interested in employing people who think traditionally.

This kind of compatibility polarizes employers into two distinct camps: enterprises that are based on a culture with characteristics consistent with the eight shared values of the new psychological contract, and enterprises exhibiting traits of the eight values of the old employment relationship. There is also a third group of employers I mentioned in Chapter 1 who are in transition between the old and new.

Table 2.3 illustrates the characteristics of this third group, sandwiched between the polar examples of the traditional and new.

Table 2.3   Values of three dominant psychological contracts

Traditional values	Transitional values	New values
Specialized employment	Some multi-skilling but mostly specialized job roles	Flexible deployment
Internal focus	Internal systems to focus on the customer, but not adequately developed	Customer focus
Job focus	Key performance indicators (KPIs) in place, but only job-related	Performance focus
Functional-based work	Some cross-functional teams, but functional departments dominate	Project-based work
Human dispirit and work	Ad-hoc strategies in place to engage employees	Human spirit and work
Loyalty	Incentives predominantly favor organizational loyalty, but some policies to enlist employee commitment	Commitment
Training	Training is largely technical, but some personal development programs	Learning and development
Closed information	Ad-hoc effort to inform employees of job and company information	Open information

I will cover in detail the two polar cultures later in this chapter. It would be useful at this stage to elaborate on the characteristics of the transitional psychological contract in the middle column. Organizations in transition from the old to the new recognize the value of flexibly deploying their staff. However, they do not yet have a comprehensive program in place that provides people with an opportunity to up-skill or multi-skill. This is therefore carried out in a piecemeal way and at the whim of management. Like most companies, enterprises in flux between the old and new are dedicated to improving their responsiveness to customers, but have all the systems and processes in place to be truly customer-focused. They understand the value of a performance-focused culture. But, these employers focus their key performance indicators (KPIs) on specific job tasks, and don't take into account KPIs in employees' non-job roles such as teamwork, innovation, and career development. They want engaged workers but have no overarching strategy in place to link their human spirit with their work. These organizations value commitment from employees and willingly reciprocate in assisting them to achieve their personal goals, although long-term loyalty is still seen as a priority over short-term commitment. Training is prominently technically-based, with some emphasis on other dimensions of learning, such as personal development. But a balanced learning and development program is yet to be put in place. Management is generally making efforts to communicate more fully with their workforce, but these efforts are not as comprehensive as they could be. People are therefore tentative about displaying initiative. Such a company is on the right path but has additional work to do to become an employer of choice.

These types of organizational culture at work offer different challenges and subsequently appeal to specific types of employee. A traditional culture will continue to attract employees who have an old-fashioned view of the employment relationship. Conversely, progressive employees find these places less appealing and, given a choice, will reject working for them. Companies such as SAS, Google, Apple, and Southwest are successful for many reasons. But one of the most important reasons for their success is their workplace culture, which reflects this new employment mindset. Companies that wholeheartedly embrace the eight new values will be more alluring to employees with similar values. At the same time, the employer of choice will be threatening to traditional workers who have an entirely different way of thinking.

What about organizations whose cultures are in transition between the old and new?

Organizational cultures in flux between the old and new will continue to send mixed signals to their current and prospective employees. As I mentioned in Chapter 1, this ambiguity and inconsistency is a significant source of confusion and frustration for employees and managers alike. Workplaces evolving from the old to the new have three choices: (1) continue on the path of uncertainty, (2) become an employer of choice with a more consistent adherence to the eight underpinning new values, or (3) move back to the simple lines of demarcation in the traditional employment relationship.

Employees have choices too, not only in terms of the kind of work they want to do, but also in terms of which culture best suits their outlook. It therefore follows that companies that aspire to being employers of choice will continue to attract and retain motivated, self-led workers with compatible value systems.

It is timely, therefore, to map out this new employment relationship mindset from the dual perspective of the individual and organization. In this way, managers, employees, trade union officials, and human resource professionals can have a clear blueprint to work towards. Gaining universal agreement is easier said than done. As we have discussed, there are many and varied vested interest groups, pressures, and traditions to retain the "them and us" relationship. But, equally, the costs of retaining and reinforcing the traditional employment relationship arguably far outweigh the benefits. Moreover, we are given the impression from popular management books and magazines that the situation is shifting faster than it really is. These superficial accounts paint an overly optimistic picture of how things are changing by citing selected cases of companies that claim to be employers of choice. While there are companies that have successfully transformed themselves into employers of choice, these are by no means as commonplace as we are led to believe.

Since the upheaval of the 1980s, with massive downsizing and outsourcing, as discussed earlier, the needs and expectations employees and employers have of each other has changed dramatically and permanently. That is why I refer to this post-1980 period as a workplace revolution. These changing expectations put considerable stress on the psychological contract.

What does the traditional employment relationship look like?

Before discussing in detail the new employment mindset needed to become an employer of choice, it would be helpful to define in more detail what I mean by the traditional employment relationship from the perspective of both the individual and the organization. The detailed description I am about to give serves three useful purposes. First, it will assist in understanding the shortcomings of this kind of relationship in coping with a fast-moving, dynamic marketplace. Second, it helps to sharpen the distinction between the old and new. Third, it gives us a set of benchmarks to measure progress towards developing a new working relationship.

At the heart of any relationship is a process of exchange between two entities. The exchange in the traditional employment relationship essentially consists of the manager specifying the work requirements and—in return for a willingness to comply—the worker receives a wage. This has been the conventional linchpin of the relationship between manager and worker since the birth of industry. Any failure to meet a work instruction, or to pay the agreed wage, means the contract collapses.

This traditional boss–worker relationship is easy to follow despite its shortcomings. It has worked successfully and has been virtually unchanged and unchallenged for a long time. Organizations that are still operating in this way are increasingly less unlikely to adjust to the challenges of a global economy. The conventional psychological contract places constraints on people. The essence of the difficulty is this: While the traditional contract is simple, people are more complicated. In this exchange process, managers are given responsibility and workers are set tasks. This creates a paradox. Employees who are not given responsibility tend to shirk responsibility and therefore never become responsible. The fewer people who take on responsibility, the greater the burden of responsibility that falls on the shoulders of the manager. However, in reality, managers can disappoint and workers can surprise others by their initiative and enterprise.

Against a backdrop of a less predictable and stable marketplace, the answer to resolving this dilemma would seem to be fairly obvious. Surely a less formal employment relationship, where managers provide workers with the freedom to be flexible and innovative in their approach to carrying out their work, is the way forward? This approach is widely advocated in many popular management books.

Unfortunately, this new approach opens the door for some employees to manipulate the system. The overlapping areas of freedom can encourage unwelcome forms of initiative being shown by political operators. For instance, employees who display appropriate initiative may be quick to take credit for this. But on the other hand, they can cite a lack of clarity as a reason for not showing enterprise when expected to by their manager. These grey areas of employee autonomy are lessened in the traditional employment contract. Put in simple terms, if it's not on the employee's job description, then it doesn't need to be done—and not doing something can be easily defended by the "work to rule" employee. Some managers undoubtedly feel threatened by a more fluid working partnership. The traditionally-minded manager, feeling insecure about a more ambiguous arrangement, will often revert to the simple separation of responsibility characterized by the "them and us" relationship. This retraction to nullifying the freedom of the employee further entrenches the traditional psychological contract.

So the test is to formulate a new working partnership with the same degree of clarity as the traditional employment relationship, without the same inflexible separation of responsibility. That sounds like a paradox too! Unlike the traditional contract, managers will not delegate and supervise tasks to the same extent. Employees are expected to take greater responsibility and to be more accountable for their output. But unless the expectations are clear and simple to both parties, any attempt to implement a new way of operating will lead to disagreement, frustration, and confusion.

The good news is that the new system I am proposing has enormous advantages for both parties. The bad news is that there is increasingly little choice for breaking the "them and us" mindset. Employees with a modern mindset are likely to seek out meaningful work, engage in continuous, lifelong learning, and assert their independence. Organizations populated with employees with these attitudes are likely to prosper. A workforce filled with independently-minded employees working on tasks they find fulfilling is a powerful competitive advantage for an enterprise. Such companies are inevitably going to lead to higher levels of productivity and responsiveness to fluctuations in market conditions.

Table 2.4 summarizes the attitudes of the traditional employment relationship from the perspective of both the employee and employer, based on eight shared values.

The left-hand column lists the eight shared values from Chapter 1 characterizing the traditional psychological contract. In the middle column, the eight descriptors are the employees' acceptable mindsets in the context of the traditional relationship. This way of thinking

Table 2.4   The Traditional Employment Relationship Model

Shared value	Employee mindset	Employer mindset
Specialized employment	Work in a clearly defined and specialized employment area	Offer clearly defined and specialized employment opportunities
Internal focus	Follow organizational policies and practices	Reinforce the need to follow organizational policies and practices
Job focus	Fulfill job requirements	Link rewards and benefits to fulfilling job requirements
Functional-based work	Focus on job functions	Structuring work around functions
Human dispirit and work	Value a stable and secure job	Offer stable and secure jobs
Loyalty	Display loyalty to the employer	Reward employees who are loyal to the organization
Training	Commitment to gain technical qualifications	Provide opportunities for employees to develop technical skills
Closed information	Comply with managerial instructions	Provide sufficient information for employees to do their job

contributes to and reinforces the eight values in the first column. The right-hand column illustrates the traditional collective outlook and the role of the employer. Here, again, these collective employer mindsets are consistent with the eight values in the first column. These employee and employer mindsets bring to life each value and also express the obligation and expectation from both entities. Should any of these responses be violated by either partner, the traditional psychological contract would be broken temporarily or permanently.

How important are values?

Values drive behavior. The values employees and employers put on their relationship determine how they act and react. For example, consider the value of loyalty, one of the shared values in the Traditional Employment Relationship Model. It is generally accepted that employees should be loyal to the boss and in return the boss provides job security to the employee. This is an important convention of the traditional psychological contract. But these days employees and employers bemoan the lack of loyalty displayed by their working partner. Employees claim that companies do not display or value loyalty of tenure anymore. Employers are frustrated that employees do not stay long enough and, after being trained up by the company, move on to greener pastures. This frustration and disappointment are based on judging behaviors against a traditional value such as loyalty.

Consider another value from the table above: the shared value of job focus. This value is based on the long-established idea that employees are given a clearly defined set of tasks to do. This is usually expressed in a job description. The job description has been used to control work performance. But this way of structuring work is more and more impractical in the modern workplace. The contemporary working landscape is becoming increasingly interdependent, flexible, and project-based as distinct from job-based. How do people break free of this emphasis on segmenting and defining work in a job description? The key is for organizational leaders to redesign organizational roles that reflect the different realities of work. For instance, these new work roles ought to be reshaped to encourage a set of attitudes recognizing, emphasizing, and reinforcing the importance of the performance of the whole workforce. Job descriptions focus on the individual. Role descriptions balance individual and organizational performance. For this shift in thinking to occur, the emphasis has to be on work people *need* to do rather than a narrowly prescribed job.

The concept of a job as we understand it is no longer applicable. Organizations need to be de-jobbed. Jobs with a clearly defined set of tasks are ill-equipped to respond to today's rapidly changing work environment. Job descriptions are inherently inflexible. For instance, the knowledge worker of today spends more time manipulating information than undertaking specific hands-on tasks. Working with information usually involves extensive liaison within and outside the workplace. In other words, information often transcends a finite set of tasks in a job statement. Consider the example of a medical professional who has a variety of sophisticated tools and technology to assist him to make a diagnosis. The work of a medical practitioner is more about interpreting data through these instruments, rather than carrying out the full task of diagnosis from a finite start and finish point. In the same way, a production worker now spends more time managing large-scale machinery than doing a specific production task itself. The emphasis of working with and through technology means that the boundaries around specific work tasks are blurred. The diagnosis from technology used by a medical analysis may, for instance, reveal symptoms beyond the scope of the medical professional. So he may need to refer the patient to another medical professional. Similarly, technology used by a production worker is likely to be interrelated with other processes beyond the scope of his/her job description. Although most organizations still value job descriptions, they are becoming obsolete.

Adding to the futility of having clearly defined job descriptions, work now increasingly crosses sections, units, departments, and divisions. People talk and collaborate with colleagues across and beyond the organization with greater frequency. What is more, they do this on a short-term basis to complete the particular project they are working on. Long-term fixed relationships in departments are giving way to short-term, temporary relationships that go beyond departmental boundaries. Job descriptions are incapable of capturing the fluidity of such work. We need to forget about jobs as we have come to know them and start thinking instead about the best way of getting the work done.

People's work is so varied that job descriptions are outdated almost as quickly as they are written. Work is not going away, but jobs are. The possibility that an individual can be employed to do a specific job with a set of detailed tasks and nothing else is unrealistic. This is why many job descriptions have a disclaimer at the bottom that goes something like this: "… and any other duties deemed necessary by your manager." The move from jobs to flexible work roles and the shift from dependent to interdependent work need to be addressed in different ways.

Segmenting an organization into departments, sections, units, or divisions does not carry the same relevance any more. Organizations are increasingly accomplishing their work through cross-functional or project teams. The rise of cross-functional work teams and the corresponding weakening of functional or departmental boundaries is occurring in response to the dynamic marketplace. There is a greater need to generate new knowledge across the enterprise. This means that in practical terms, information—more than ever—has to be shared beyond departmental boundaries. Rapid changes in the marketplace require a rapid response. And that means distributing information across the organization at a faster rate. It's unsurprising, therefore, that self-directed work teams (SDWTs) are now becoming the basic organizational work unit.

Typically, the individual employee now receives a task "bundle" that is to be accomplished by a team in a holistic fashion whereas, before, employees would be issued specific tasks to do as individuals. Individuals working in SDWTs, doing whatever needs to be done to make the business a success, represent the new entrepreneurial model.

On the surface, the evolving workplace signals losses for the organization and individual. Employees have lost job security and a sense of long-term organizational identity. Companies, on the other hand, have lost the predictability of managing a dependent and internally-orientated workforce.

What alternatives are available to traditional ways of dividing up work?

Organizations that will thrive in this new reality are those that will be filled with employees who have the option to leave, but choose to stay because of the work. Companies that fail to grasp this will increasingly be populated by employees who are there only because they are afraid to go elsewhere. A new model is essential to replace the one that relies on job segmentation.

Much of the unrest in workplaces today can be attributed to the conflicting expectations employers and managers have of each other. This can even be found within a company. For instance, managers want and need employees to take more responsibility for their work. But, at the same time, managers have traditionally focused almost entirely on organizational outputs. This is traditionally what leaders have been measured against. This output focus has often been at the expense of employee growth. Employees generally want managers to provide them with more say in the day-to-day running of the business. But other employees with a traditional view of their work may believe that managers are paid to make decisions and workers are paid to follow instructions. These conflicting viewpoints of the psychological contract create misunderstandings and confusion between managers and employees. Today's workplaces are filled with these paradoxes. These misinterpretations are clear indicators that a transformation is underway.

Managers who understand and encourage this shift away from job demarcation to a more integrated model will continue to be in greater demand. Progressive leaders who promote interdependence and the expectations that go with this approach will be able to recruit and retain top talent and build an enlightened workplace. Employers of choice are able to attract and retain self-led employees who share these values needed for success.

Self-motivated employees who have a modern appreciation of the changing world of work are also increasingly in demand. Various statistics suggest that approximately one-third of employees in the current marketplace are contingent and self-employed. With a greater demand for more independent workers, fewer employees will be in fixed, long-term, traditional jobs. The implications for managing an increasingly itinerant workforce, on the one hand, and learning to be an itinerant worker on the other, go beyond the confines of the traditional psychological contract. A new mindset is necessary for organizational leaders to assist employees in mastering the portable career skills needed for the twenty-first century. In exchange, employees who commit to, and embrace, a spirit of competitive urgency and continuous learning will most likely respond favorably.

In Chapter 3, we look at the traditional way people are developed, to prepare them to be better workers. Traditional learning and development strategies are a big impediment to fostering a new approach. Specifically, traditional learning and development approaches actually reinforce the traditional mindset. Without rethinking the way people develop, the human resource development industry will become a dinosaur and continue to slow the pace of change.

The **10** Key Points ...

1. The workplace revolution commenced with the massive layoffs of the 1980s; people lost trust in the traditional employment relationship and the era of globalization took off.

2. The "them and us" employment relationship is a relic of the past century and is unsuitable for a rapidly changing and uncertain marketplace.

3. A successful career in the twentieth century was based on a secure job, qualifications, and expressed loyalty to the organization. In the twenty-first century, these pillars are totally opposite; they are employability, continuous learning, and independence respectively.

4. Successful organizations in the twentieth century were based on characteristics such as quality systems and processes, career paths for employees, and a loyal staff. In the twenty-first century, these traits are entirely different and include customer responsiveness, engaged staff, and a focus on commitment.

5. Three dominant psychological contracts are segmenting the marketplace. The transition between the old and new contracts will lead to confusion and frustration because they are sending out mixed signals.

6. The traditional psychological contract is based on eight shared values: specialist employment, internal focus, job focus, functional-based work, human dispirit and work, loyalty, training, and closed information.

7. Values are important: they drive behavior.

8   Job descriptions are now obsolete.

9   The progressive manager who promotes independence rather than job demarcation will be appealing for recruiting and retaining top talent and building an enlightened workplace.

10 The employment relationship is a process of exchange between employee and employer.

chapter 3

Does the HRD Industry Have a Future?

> *I don't know about you, but I don't think of myself as a "human resource" or "human capital": I am a human being!*

Jeanette is an HR manager with a traditional approach to HRD. She refers to staffing matters as human resource matters; her training budget is almost entirely spent on technical and competence-based training. She wants employees to learn, follow, and be accountable for sticking to the organizational manual. In fact, she judges her success by how compliant people are in following organizational systems and processes. When a dilemma arises, she wants them to refer to the comprehensive manual she calls "The Bible," and follow policies and procedures to the letter. Jeanette has been described as a transactional leader, and she is proud of that description. Her paperwork is impeccably completed and she values observance and risk aversion. She is hands-on and buries herself in the detail of an issue. She wants and seeks out all the facts. Jeanette does not ask many questions but prides herself on answering questions and giving the "right" answer. Training is usually done formally in a classroom with a trainer referring to a set training manual. Good training, in her mind, is following and getting through the training workbook before the end of the time allotted. Managers, in her mind, are there to lead and make decisions.

Craig replaced her as HR manager and had an entirely different approach to learning and development. He changed the name of the department to

"People, Performance and Well-being." Craig changed the training agenda and introduced such courses as lateral thinking and problem solving; he put more emphasis on personal development. Craig thought the main thrust of his role was about changing the culture of the organization and put in place a plan to launch the company on the road to becoming an employer of choice. He left operational matters to line managers, whom Craig thought were in the best position to deal with day-to-day matters. Much to the frustration of consultants who had a good relationship with Craig's predecessor, they were asked by Craig to shorten their sessions and break the program into smaller chunks. The trainers were used to coming in and running one-day programs and riding off into the sunset afterwards. He spent his first few weeks talking to employees who were at the coalface. Craig wanted to understand the challenges they faced in their jobs.

One of the major impediments to developing a culture based on a new mindset about the employment relationship is the traditional way that people are managed within organizations. Approaches to HRD have generally failed to keep pace with the workplace revolution. Conventional responses to learning and development are no longer relevant in a fast-paced climate. A new way forward for HRD is long overdue. The Jeanettes of the world are becoming obsolete. We need more Craigs!

What's wrong with HRD?

You have probably picked up that I am critical of much of the material available on HRD and change management because it fails to understand the importance of changing tack, or to appreciate how the evolving psychological contract has dramatically changed the role of HRD. Instead of helping, I would go so far as saying that most approaches to change management and HRD actually hinder business development and, in so doing, are damaging businesses and the people that populate them. Despite all the rhetoric, much of the change and human development practices are—at the very least—holding businesses and employees back from realizing their full potential. These popular programs come and go. As I point out in my book, *The End of the Performance Review: A New Approach to Appraising Employee Performance,*[1] approaches such as process re-engineering, downsizing, upsizing, rightsizing, and so on are replacing each other because they are ineffective and unsustainable attempts at meeting the necessities of organizations operating in this rapidly changing global environment. Conventional HRD is obsessed with competencies, skills development, and implementing and following processes and procedures. These strategies are essentially about doing, applying, or improving something within the business; they do not question the underlying assumptions of the way people work together.

More than ever, what organizations really need is a set of strategic initiatives that confront and deal with the mindsets employer and employee have of their relationship. It is difficult to argue with the notion that changing people's thinking is the cornerstone for changing their behavior. As I suggested in the previous chapter, values drive behavior. Conventional HRD practices are still operating from pre-1980s thinking. As the title of this chapter suggests, I think that if HRD doesn't radically modify its thinking, it risks irrelevancy in the near future.

To address the changing learning and development requirements in today's world, managers everywhere are using a variety of strategies to involve and "empower" employees. These approaches are promoted by most popular management authors. Studies carried out in different countries confirm a rise in the proportion of companies implementing approaches to get their staff more involved in day-to-day decision making. This technique is commonly referred to as "empowerment." There are many ways to empower

---

[1] Baker, T.B. (2013) *The End of the Performance Review: A New Approach to Appraising Employee Performance.* London: Palgrave Macmillan (or purchase from www.winnersatwork.com.au).

employees, according to the HRD experts. But these approaches, more often than not, leave managers frustrated and disillusioned. They scratch their heads and wonder why they don't work. In their disenchantment, managers often revert to the command and control management tactic.

Many of these attempted empowerment tactics involve a different communication style, such as briefing teams on a more regular basis, inviting suggestions for improvement, and collaborative problem solving. While the use of these methods is growing, most of these techniques are just that: techniques. They are applied in an ad hoc manner and their impact is fairly superficial. In most cases, these techniques do not challenge the core conventions of the old employment relationship. They are done in the interest of the organization, rather than the interest of the persons being empowered. Their main feature is to involve employees in owning their job so that they can take a personal interest in improving the performance of the organization. The concept sounds great—in principle. But, despite the way it is promoted, it is really about the company and not the person.

Until the HRD industry gets to grips with the dynamics of psychological contracts, practitioners will be continually looking for the latest and greatest new approach. There is nothing inherently wrong with the idea of empowering people. In fact, it is a great idea. But it will not be sustainable when empowerment techniques are introduced against the backdrop of the "them and us" workplace culture. Managers often use the tactic of empowerment to change the traditional command and control culture, a characteristic of the traditional employment relationship. But empowerment, being a forward-thinking tactic, will have trouble gaining traction in a culture underpinned by a conventional psychological contract.

To fulfill their potential as change agents, the architects of such HRD approaches need to genuinely balance individual and organizational interests. In short, HRD professionals ought to look for the common ground. Many of these tools—as good as they are in isolation—are employer-centric and fail to take proper account of the interests of the people they are attempting to change. Most HRD practices either do not address the issue of potentially conflicting expectations between management and labor, or assume there is a commonality of interests. While managers are losing faith in the practical application of these tools, employees are becoming more skeptical of the motives behind these change strategies, knowing that the real motive is to benefit the organization. For instance, most change management strategies are "top-down" models, driven by organizational leaders without proper engagement of employees. So it is little wonder that employees are suspicious of these "strategic initiatives." We need genuinely collaborative approaches that involve both managers and employees in the process of change.

Further, employees are often asked to apply outdated models and processes to develop new workplace skills. For instance, most of the training and development models available today presume a predictable, certain, and straightforward working environment. But, as we all know, modern work environments are characterized by increasing speed and ambiguity. This means that people are increasingly facing new and unusual problems and challenges to deal with. Consider this: Have you ever gone up to a hotel's reception desk and asked for something a bit out of the ordinary, such as the recipe for the meal you enjoyed the night before? It's an unusual, but not unreasonable, request. The receptionist looks panicked. S/he is probably thinking, "I haven't been trained to deal with this request. It's not in the manual under the desk." The front office person has been trained to follow standard operating procedures, not to solve problems or think laterally. So their training when these situations arise is counterproductive: they feel helpless and disempowered. As work is becoming less prescriptive and predictable, this places new and unique pressures and demands on service providers.

So the way we develop people at work is now due for an overhaul. Employees have to be agile in their thinking when dealing with these kinds of predicaments. They are now called upon to add, replace, enhance, and retrofit their capabilities to suit the environment. It is paradoxical, on the one hand, that most organizational leaders understand the importance and value of employees being flexible and adaptable in certain situations. But, on the other hand, managers expect employees to follow standard operating practices in other circumstances. This dual expectation can be confusing for employees. New HRD models that promote initiative and independent thinking often go against the ethos of traditional "paint by numbers" training.

Present models of training and development originated in the military. Conventional HRD is modeled on a training instructional system. I acknowledge that HRD has evolved somewhat from the instructional approach, but developing work expertise is still mostly prescriptive and determinant. These static and linear training models still have their place, but they are unlikely to be effective in developing the type of skilled performance needed in an increasingly contingent and dynamic work environment.

Another important feature of the changing workplace that challenges the HRD profession is the shift from technical capacity to human development. The strategic potential to build capacity in companies is moving beyond factors such as production and process technology, economies of scale, financial resources or protecion, and regulated markets. The competitive advantages are increasingly in the adequate deployment and management of people. Employees should be viewed as an investment needing careful attention, rather than a cost factor that needs to be reduced. People are now central to business success. In keeping with this changing emphasis, the primary focus of HRD ought to be squarely on developing the creative potential of employees. The military-inspired model of process mastery training is less relevant than it used to be.

The idea that "people are the most important resource in our business" may well be a cliché, but it is increasingly the case. Both public- and private-sector organizations are depending more and more on fewer and fewer people. With the reality of a wider array of problems to confront and fewer available resources, the HRD profession needs to rethink how employees are utilized, developed, resourced, and motivated.

Further, the concept of how productivity is achieved has changed. The focus of any business is still about maximizing income and at the same time minimizing expenses; in short, it is about making a profit. But the way this is achieved is evolving. The dominant forces for productive gain in the past were largely financial capital and technical superiority. While these factors are still important, the dimension of human capital is even more important. Financial and technical resources are now—more than ever—accessible to an ever-increasing number of entrepreneurs. The commoditization of financial capital and technical know-how levels the playing field, so to speak. Human capital and how it is deployed is now the key driver of productivity. Developing human capital to realize its full potential is paramount to business success.

Jobs are increasingly being shaped more by the qualities of the people performing them. Status and compensation are more and more attached to people, not positions. A workforce that is highly skilled, motivated, and adaptive is the order of the day. Productivity is linked to a workforce that has the opportunity to express its full talent and potential. Enabling, encouraging, and rewarding employees to fulfill their potential is more important than ever.

Learning over the past thirty years has progressively been recognized as a critical factor in commercial advantage. The company's ability to learn and innovate is increasingly being seen as having a positive impact on revenues, profit, and economic value. Learning is also viewed as a way of penetrating new markets and achieving sustained market leadership. Applied learning can enhance speed and innovation.

Why is speed so important?

Speed has a direct relationship to productivity. It is a fundamental measure of organizational efficiency and effectiveness. There are three types of speed that organizations need in order to be productive.[2]

Innovative speed

Innovative speed means being in the marketplace first with the goods and services that customers want and need. Speed, in this sense, is about constantly innovating and experimenting with new features that give the customer what they desire, before a company runs the risk of losing them to a competitor. Product life cycles are getting shorter. First-mover advantage will continue to become more and more significant. Innovation speed is directly related to agility: being agile means taking advantage of opportunities as they arise. An obvious example of this is Apple and their speed to market of touch-screen technology. Although it is largely commonplace now, this was not the case when the iPhone was first released onto the market. Being first to market was a huge advantage to the company and, consequently, led to enormous revenues in a short time frame. Being innovative is virtually impossible when people are trained to comply with organizational systems and processes.

---

[2] Kanter, R.M. (1995) "Mastering change," in S. Chawla & J. Renesch (eds), *Learning Organizations: Developing Cultures for Tomorrow's Workplace* (pp. 71–83). Portland, OR: Productivity Press.

Processing speed

Processing speed means administering everything through the organization as quickly as possible and faster than competitors. For instance, this refers to such things as shortening cycle times for designing training programs, restructuring companies, and implementing new products and services. The processing of applications for approving finances for an investment property—for example—can give a banking or finance company an edge over their competitors. Processing speed give a company a considerable advantage over their rivals. Improving the speed of processes means that employees ought to be encouraged to question the status quo: Why are we doing things this way? Is there a better, faster way of administering this transaction? Here, again, conventional learning and development practices train people largely to accept things as they are.

Recovery speed

Recovery speed refers to the time it takes to respond to and fix problems. For instance, a fundamental tenet of superior customer service is how quickly a company can put right a mistake it has made and rectify the situation. Customers are often forgiving if they feel their issue is being dealt with as a priority in a speedy way. Holding on to these customers and not losing them to a rival is the aim. Recovery speed is based on the assumption that mistakes will happen—and they do—and, in these circumstances, fixing them quickly is the best outcome for everyone. This requires people to be enterprising and use their initiative, qualities not valued in conventional learning programs.

When you take into account these three types of speed, you can see the need for speed as an enabler of productivity. Speed is dependent on a high degree of organizational adaptability. Companies that are faster moving are also more flexible in how they deploy their workforce. This requires a different way of developing people and their capacities.

Companies that demonstrate consistently high levels of innovation, processing, and recovery speed have agile workforces. These are workforces where employees have broader definitions of their job. In many occupations, being versatile in dealing with varying demands and situations is more highly valued than working hard in a single activity. For instance, for someone in a sales role, dealing thoughtfully and empathetically with a customer complaint, rather than chasing new business, requires a comprehensive appreciation of their organizational role. In quite a few cases this adaptability can be considered in retrospect, as a better investment of time than looking for new sales leads. Training employees to be adaptable can assist them to make better decisions.

As I pointed out in Chapter 2, cross-functional work teams are another HRD process for improving adaptability in the workplace. Modern managers, in their quest for organizational flexibility, create project teams that bridge functions and departments. Companies that move faster, innovate quickly, progress things through the organization without haste, and solve problems immediately are more likely to be organized around cross-functional teams. Cross-functional structures bring people together across departments to tackle something new or to solve a company-wide problem. In contrast, hierarchical organizational structures slow the pace of decision making.

Learning, speed, and flexibility support a new approach to enhancing productivity and these dimensions present new challenges for HRD. Productivity, conceptualized in this way, relies heavily on people's capacity to demonstrate enterprising behavior in their work. Being enterprising is about innovation and taking risks rather than accuracy and precision. This shift in thinking provides new challenges and opportunities for HRD.

What does HRD need to do differently?

Table 3.1 summarizes the changes that are needed for HRD to respond to the issues I have outlined.

The left-hand column identifies seven HRD concepts. These concepts, or themes, provide the basis for understanding the conventional and future paradigms about HRD. There are undoubtedly more themes to consider for HRD, but these are a useful starting point for a discussion on what HRD needs to change. The middle column summarizes the conventional response for each of the seven concepts, and the right-hand column summarizes the appropriate new responses to the seven themes. The responses in the right-hand column are consistent with the changing world of work. By embracing this new paradigm, HRD will continue to have an effective role to play in the twenty-first century.

I will explain each of these concepts and paradigm shifts below.

Branding

"Human resources" is a derogatory term. It implies that people are the captive possessions of organizations. Many writers use another term: human capital. Although a little more palatable, I do not see

Table 3.1   The changing paradigms of HRD

Concept	Conventional HRD	Future HRD
Branding	Human resources	People
Learning emphasis	Doing	Thinking
Type of learning	Training	Problem solving
Orientation to HRD	Maintaining the status quo	Managing change
Focus	Operational focus	Strategic focus
Approach to learning	Linear	Cyclical
Strategy	Top-down approach	Bottom-up approach

myself as either a *human resource* or *human capital*. The rebranding of HR departments and HRD sends an important signal that their business is really about people, their performance, well-being, and development. Human resource departments are now changing their branding to reflect this reality. However, many organizations still use the term "human resources" without questioning it. Rebranding to reflect the fact that HR is really about people is an important first step in changing the paradigm of HRD.

The term *resources* implies that people are the property of the organization where they work. Are people resources in the same way that organizations own administrative and technical resources? In terms of the traditional employment relationship, the answer would be yes. But I think there has been a positive shift in the last thirty years, away from the idea that people are owned by organizations. For instance, the basic premise of the downsizing movement of the 1980s was to cut costs in companies. Some people were viewed as liabilities. They were seen as business costs, arguably no different to any other costs of doing business. Describing employees as human resources was apt then: it described the way people were viewed by business owners. Of course, some employers today still view employees as no more than a necessary cost of doing business. Since then, the term *human capital* has become popular. Human capital also implies employer ownership over people, albeit in a more positive light. Consistent with the new psychological contract, the HRD profession should view employees as free agents who offer their services to organizations in exchange for benefits.

Learning emphasis

HRD has been obsessed with what people do, rather than how they think. Conventional HRD has been preoccupied with the pursuit and development of competencies. These competencies are usually about the technical aspects of jobs. But achieving technical competence does not directly address the need to change the way people think about their organizational role. Behavior change is unlikely to happen in any sustainable way without the right mindset in place. For example, teaching people planning techniques is unlikely to be practiced in an organization that has a culture of "flying by the seat of its pants" (see the vignette at the beginning of Chapter 1). While a learning program may teach people a series of useful planning techniques, they are unlikely to use them if they do not believe they can be used in their current working environment. Tackling the reasons why people value spontaneity over planning in this case would be a constructive first step towards changing the necessary behavior. HRD ought to be in the business of directly changing the way people think, as a prerequisite for changing their work practices.

By getting people to think differently, I am not suggesting a form of brainwashing. I am not implying that, by changing people's thinking, we indoctrinate people for manipulative purposes. What's more, fresh thinking can benefit the individual and organization. If a learner does not embrace new ways of thinking to accompany a new competency, the learning experience may not be successful. For example, it is no use teaching someone how to write good reports unless the learner understands why it is important and how it will benefit them and the organization they work in. Behavior change is the basis of any effective learning program. In order to change a person's behavior, you pretty much need to change the way they think. Conventional learning focuses on skill development; it underestimates the importance and value of changing the way people think. Changing the learner's attitude is often bypassed on the assumption that the trainee already understands the context and value of the learning exercise, or will recognize it sooner or later.

Type of learning

Most HRD programs are about training people to improve their technical skills and competencies. They have a heavy emphasis on the transfer of content from an "expert" to the "students." Yet, in a climate of rapid change and uncertainty, equipping people with the skills to critically reflect and solve problems is vital to help them cope with the increasing array of demands they will face in their work. As I pointed out in Chapter 2, the complexity of problems facing employees and the ever-changing landscape is placing greater pressure and demands on people to think quickly and often differently. For instance, customers are undoubtedly becoming more demanding and varied in their preferences: I know I am! Customers have more choices. Sales and marketing frontline staff are often called upon by more demanding customers to think "outside the box." Problem-based learning is often neglected in favor of a formulaic approach that assumes we are still operating in the stable and predictable environment of the twentieth century.

I discuss problem-based learning in more detail in Chapter 11. However, in the interests of clarity, I will briefly explain the concept here. Problem-based learning covers a wide array of topics. It essentially interacts with a realistic work-based case, developing fresh insights through analysis and discovery. Apart from learning new ways of thinking about a problem, improvements in team and communication skills often result from problem-based learning, since it is regularly carried out in teams or groups. Using problem-based—rather than prescriptive—learning, people become more nimble at processing information and developing practical skills that can be applied to unanticipated problems and challenges encountered at work.

Orientation to HRD

Most conventional HRD interventions are designed and carried out to uphold and maintain core workplace processes and practice. I acknowledge that learning and reinforcing certain tried and proven practices is still important in many instances, such as health and safety and recruitment. However, prescriptive training is not helpful in fostering innovation and continuous improvement. More emphasis should to be placed on equipping people with the capacity to cope with and initiate change. Also, giving employees the skills and mindsets to question the current way things are being done is valuable both for employees and the workplace.

Change management programs are too focused on process and not enough on people. More specifically, conventional change management programs stress the importance of steps and phases: they do not usually concentrate enough attention on managing people through change. Instead, these well-meaning courses are usually about how to manage situations with outdated techniques or tactics. Many fail to take into account the psychological responses to change and how these reactions ought to be managed. When these programs do concentrate on people's reactions to change, they are dominated by strategies on overcoming employee resistance. While I acknowledge that resistance is a real emotional response to change, so too are many other reactions, such as denial, exploration, and commitment. These programs assume that resistance is the only emotion that people experience in a change process. At any rate, the HRD profession is slow to develop more sophisticated approaches to change and still too concerned with preserving the status quo.

Focus

A fair chunk of conventional learning and development initiatives are designed to improve the operational capacity of the organization. This operational focus includes the majority of technical training. Although increasing, HRD ought to focus on the strategic dimension of the organization. Strategic learning and development assist the organization to achieve its corporate vision. At the very least, HR needs to articulate a very clear link between operational skills development and the strategic direction of the organization. If HR professionals want more influence in the boardroom, they should frame their case for training programs in business terms so that senior non-HR executives are sold on the benefits to the business. More effort to align HRD with the organizational vision is likely to legitimize the relevance of organizational learning and development initiatives.

Too much HRD is still carried out in isolation without connecting the learning to the strategic goals of the organization. From my observations, people working in the HR function of a business should put a lot more energy into selling the value of what they do in the context of helping the enterprise move closer to its goals. As challenging as it surely is, emphasizing the return on investment of any learning program is important. It addresses the question: How will this learning experience help the participants move closer to achieving the charter of the organization? In short, all HRD initiatives must be seen through the lens of the organization's vision.

Approach to learning

Most learning and development programs still have fixed start and finish dates. In other words, the program is a single event rather than an ongoing process of development. For example, a one-day training program usually requires participates to arrive in the morning. Over the day, they undertake a predetermined series of learning activities and finish that afternoon. This is often referred to as the "sheep dipping" approach; that is, everyone gets the same information in the same way at the same time. These one-off training programs do have their place, but a more effective approach to learning is an enduring process that is flexible and adaptive to learners' emerging needs. This approach is commonly referred to as *action learning*. An action learning approach identifies issues that require development. The learning experience is prepared and tailored to the needs of the learner. The learning is undertaken using a multidimensional approach. Its effectiveness in behavior change is then evaluated. From the evaluation, modifications are made and the learning experience continues. Its emphasis is cyclical, rather than linear. This recurring approach is in keeping with the well-founded learning principles of spaced and continuous learning.

By approaching learning and development in a cyclical fashion, HRD becomes a seamless part of the organization's day-to-day activities. Learning experiences are less formal, shorter, more frequent, and practically based. This approach is in direct contrast to the majority of programs, which are isolated occurrences where employees typically "down tools" and head for the training room for a day of absorbing content from a set program outline and workbook. During the breaks, people dash outside to catch up on email and other work-related matters. Training done this way is often viewed by the participants as a distraction from the work that they still have to do. Action learning as an approach is more in keeping with a rapidly changing workplace.

Strategy

Conventional wisdom suggests that the top-down approach is the only effective way to bring about organizational change. However, this traditional approach to change is based on two potentially faulty assumptions. First, the top-down strategy implies that top management knows best. Sometimes they do; sometimes they don't. Second, most top-down models are driven by organizational leaders without regard for the strategic involvement of employees at all levels of the organizational structure. The effectiveness of the bottom-up approach to bring about powerful and prolonged change, sadly, is underestimated.

Change initiatives from the bottom up are based on an opposite set of assumptions. First, that a variety of perspectives can—if managed properly—enhance the decision-making process. Second, people generally want to feel they are part of the development of the organization. Leaders still initiate the change process using the bottom-up approach, but do so in a collaborative way, thereby involving the people directly affected by the change. The bottom-up approach to change requires more consultation, greater emphasis on selling the need for change, and earlier planning and execution. In contrast, the top-down approach is usually characterized by the opposite: a lack of consultation, failure to explain the need for change, and rushed implementation. The outcome is more often than not confusing and lacking in genuine buy-in. Bottom-up approaches to organizational development initiatives have a more important role to play than is currently evidenced in organizations.

These seven changing paradigms are more in keeping with the changing psychological contract shown in the right-hand column of Table 3.1. There is still a place for conventional HRD strategies, but the emphasis needs to be on these new strategic approaches. If it is, HRD is likely to enhance its effectiveness and legitimacy and be a facilitator of a culture that values and reinforces the new employment relationship. And as we have discussed, this shift in emphasis will be attractive to current and potential employees.

What is desperately needed, not only by the HRD industry but business in general, is a new and radically different paradigm for learning and development. A new model for HRD adds to its legitimacy in the boardroom, enhances its effectiveness, can create a new culture, and is in keeping with the changing times.

Before we go any further, I would like to consider what is meant by a productive organizational culture and the role of HRD in creating an attractive organizational culture.

What is organizational culture?

Most managers are aware that a positive workplace culture is likely to lead to higher levels of productivity and, equally, an inappropriate, or negative, culture tends to result in lower levels of productivity.

Although managers generally understand and appreciate this connection between organizational culture and productivity, they are not too sure where and how to start the process of changing the organization's culture. As I have mentioned already, managers have used ad hoc HRD approaches that sidestep the employer/employee relationship. Organizational culture is largely a by-product of the engagement between employee and employer. Transforming the culture of a company from an old employment mindset to the new employment collaboration provides the foundation for an increase in sustainable productivity.

It is difficult to find a universally accepted definition of organizational culture. Fundamentally, organizational culture is the personality of the organization. Every organization—whether public or private—has one. Culture is difficult to express distinctly and has many dimensions; however, everyone knows what it is when they see it. Organizational culture is an ambiguous term. In plain English, organizational culture is the "way things are done around here." And the way things are done in an organizational setting is mainly a reflection of the relationship between employee and employer.

From Enron to Google, corporate culture says a lot about an organization's character, influencing how it's perceived by customers, employees, and competitors alike. A positive organizational culture may express itself through happy and secure employees in a friendly environment, while a negative one may be characterized by overworked employees or ill-defined roles and responsibilities. Regardless of the specifics, culture can usually be found in a company's overall philosophy and how it reflects on workplace dynamics, particularly in the relationship between managers and employees. In explicit ways, corporate culture dictates the dress code, hours worked, approach to employee training and development, on-site perks, interactions between workers and management, the arrangement of work space, and the general impression of being in a hostile or welcoming environment.

The final impact of organizational culture is more than just employee satisfaction; it can has a significant effect on a company's bottom line. According to McKinsey,[3] a well-known international management consultancy, in 2009, cultural factors accounted for more than 70 percent of obstacles that prevent a business from reaching its performance improvement goals: 33 percent of barriers involved management behavior that does not support change and 39 percent were due to employee reluctance to accept innovation. Competitors can quickly mimic a successful strategy. What they cannot replicate quickly is a superior performance culture.

When you think of Google as a company, what words come to mind? Most people would use words like "flexibility," "innovation," and "fun corporate culture." Now think of words that describe a typical government department. Most people would use opposite words, such as "stable," "dependable" (maybe!), and "rigid." Every organization has its own cultural branding. Some are successful because they are flexible, adaptable, customer-focused, engaging, committed, and open. Others are known for their inflexibility, internal focus, disengagement of staff, lack of commitment, and closed communication channels. These cultural characteristics can permeate every aspect of the workplace.

Understanding your own organization's culture is important. That culture will affect the decisions you make either as a manager or employee, the processes you want to implement or carry out, and the results you can expect from your boss or your teams. Classifying a workplace's culture is not as easy as it sounds. For instance, if I asked you to think of the organization you work in as a color, animal, and vehicle, what would you say, and why? For example, you might say gold, because we strive to be number one; cheetah, because we are fast moving; and Ferrari, because we are

---

[3] At http://news.thomasnet.com/IMT/2009/06/23/whats-your-corporate-culture-organization-customer-employee-business-relations/, accessed January 2014.

top of the range. On the other hand, you might say grey, because we are nothing special; elephant, because we are slow to change; and old van, because we are always breaking down. Others working with you may have a different perspective. I encourage you to try this exercise with your staff. People working side by side can have different perceptions of their workplace. Compare notes.

If I then asked you to describe the color, animal, and vehicle you would like your workplace culture to be, what would you say and why? Are your answers different? I would imagine they would be different unless you are fortunate enough to be working for an employer of choice. How can you get from A to B? Before getting to B you must know what B is and how far it is from A. The right corporate culture is important for a variety of reasons.

As I mentioned at the beginning of Chapter 1, Eric Schmidt, executive chairman of Google, describes his company's culture as their competitive advantage. He claims that Google's culture is their main leverage over Microsoft. Microsoft's culture is also strong, though very different from Google's. Creating a favorable workplace culture can differentiate you from your competitors. To a certain extent, it can insulate your business from competition. Your competitors can copy your products, services, and processes—but it is much harder for your competitors to copy your culture. There are few companies who can call their culture a competitive edge. Regrettably, most employers and employees see their culture as holding them back in some way, and are desperately trying—often with little success—to change it.

For Google, the cultural challenge is how to preserve their culture as they grow bigger. As the recent financial crisis hit, and advertising revenues fell, Google faced the test of how to keep their employee-centric culture while simultaneously making across-the-board expenses cuts for the first time in their history. They had to distinguish between the values of employee-centricity and the perks which they had always given to employees. Google were quick to make drastic cuts to their budget within days of the crisis, but these cuts did not occur in employee benefits. The cuts were clean, sharp, and clear, demonstrating that accountability and employee-centricity can go hand in hand. Their results[4] coming out of the crisis showed Google emerging even stronger, and focused on the future. They demonstrate that once you have built a strong culture, one that balances the needs of both the employee and employer, you have a deposit of trust between both parties. The leadership has "walked their talk" for a long time, and people know that. Sending a message that employee benefits have to be cut, or the workforce reduced, is accepted within a context of a strong culture and a financial crisis. But without strong shared values, such decisions are met with cynicism and even hostility.

There is a reason that the same companies regularly appear on the list of Fortune's "100 Best Companies to Work For." As well as ranking among the best providers of customer service and topping profitability standings, a positive organizational culture elevates standards across the board. As James Heskett and Earl Sasser, authors of *The Ownership Quotient*, point out, an organization with a clearly codified organizational culture can expect the following benefits:

- A better place to work;
- The company will be well known among prospective employees;
- A high level of ownership (e.g., referral rates and ideas for improving the business from existing employees);
- A simplified screening process, as employees tend to refer similar-minded acquaintances;
- A larger pool of prospective employees; and
- An effective hiring process, with fewer mismatches.

---

[4] At http://isedb.com/20091019-2155/googles-third-quarter-results-released-pleasing-but-not-stellar/, accessed January 2014.

Corporate culture depends on many factors beyond a mission statement or business model. Too many organizations assume they know what their culture is. Often they think that it can be summed up in a slogan, such as "We have a culture of innovation" or "We're an action-based culture." Others assume their values statement adequately represents their unique culture. It does not. At the heart of organizational culture is the way that management and the workforce relate to each other.

Companies with cultures that have proven successful, such as Southwest Airlines, with its upbeat approach to flying, or Google, with its reputation for openness and creativity, can serve as examples of the power of a positive culture. They are employers of choice because of their corporate culture. But their approaches should not necessarily serve as a template. Each company has a unique culture, and careful assessment can help identify the areas that need improvement as well as the particular strategy that would work for a specific firm.

At any rate, an optimistic and productive corporate culture can allow a company to reap major benefits and, perhaps most importantly, it perpetuates itself by attracting the best talent. Given the option between coming to an open and engaging workplace every day or merely showing up for a job, which would you choose? That is the central question employers of choice focus on. You want to attract top performers and keep them engaged for longer than would normally be the case. And if you are a top performer with options, you know which workplace you would choose.

What is the role of HRD in organizational culture?

HRD has a critical role in shaping the culture of a workplace. It can reinforce a traditional culture, on the one hand, or create the dynamics for a progressive culture on the other. I started this chapter by asking the question: Does the HRD industry have a future? I think it does, provided it is willing to change direction, as I explained earlier. If HRD is prepared to focus on people, rather than "human resources," that would be a great start. If HRD devotes more energy to changing people's thinking, this will lead to more sustainable results. If HRD adopts problem-based learning rather than using off-the-shelf learning solutions, people will be more adaptive and responsive. If HRD focuses on change and assisting people to cope with this, it will make the organization more robust. If HRD is more strategic and links learning and development to business goals, it will legitimize its existence. If HRD takes a more continuous improvement approach to learning, it will create organizational capacity. If HRD gets the genuine buy-in of workforces, it will achieve so much more, and will last longer. That is a lot of "ifs"! There is no doubt that, by embracing a new paradigm for developing people, organizations have a powerful vehicle to create the employer of choice culture I have been speaking about.

Chapter 4 introduces the New Employment Relationship Model and explains how it can be used as a roadmap towards becoming an employer of choice. If HRD can align their thinking with this model, it is a useful starting point for creating a desirable organizational culture.

The **10** Key Points …

One of the major impediments to developing a culture based on a new mindset about the employment relationship is the traditional way that people are developed within organizations.

Until the HRD industry gets to grips with the dynamics of psychological contracts, practitioners will continually be looking for the latest, greatest new approaches that are unsustainable ways of changing culture.

3. Present models of training and development originated in the military and are increasingly ineffective.

4. The idea that "people are the most important resource in our business" may well be a cliché, but it is increasingly the case.

5. Speed has a direct relationship to productivity. Organizations need three types of speed in order to be productive: innovation, processing, and recovery.

6. Companies that demonstrate consistently high levels of speed innovation have agile workforces.

7. The concepts of learning, speed, and flexibility support a new definition of productivity and present new challenges for HRD.

8. A new model for HRD adds to its legitimacy in the boardroom, enhances its effectiveness, can create a new culture, and is in keeping with the changing times.

9. The final impact of organizational culture is more than just employee satisfaction: it can also be seen to significantly affect the bottom line.

10. HRD has a critical role in shaping the culture of a workplace.

The New Employment
Relationship Model

This individual/organization interface can be likened to the "yin and yang" relationship. In a yin/yang relationship, the halves need each other to create a unified whole.

SAS is the leader in business analytics software and services, and the largest independent vendor in the business intelligence market. Through innovative solutions delivered within an integrated framework, SAS helps customers at more than 50,000 sites to improve performance and deliver value by making better decisions faster.

SAS is among the top 35 companies in Italy, according to the Great Place to Work® Institute, a research company specializing in analyzing workplaces. U.S.-based SAS—a privately held company—pays particular attention to the individual and the balance between work and personal life. SAS also treats sustainability as a serious, core value, not simply a question of image. The difference is well understood by employees, both in Italy and at corporate head office, where SAS topped Fortune magazine's "100 Best Companies to Work For" list in the United States in 2010 and 2011.

For SAS Italy, attention to the workplace environment is a comprehensive strategy that puts people at the center. With three hundred employees, *they have been able to create an environment in which they can work more comfortably and be more productive.*

Building a personalized approach for each employee might mean, for example, making intelligent use of flexible working hours or telecommuting. It also involves designing a growth plan to identify personal and professional development opportunities. SAS also strives to help employees with their everyday needs: SAS is one of few companies in Italy to provide employees with a "company butler," who can help with miscellaneous tasks such as paying bills or running errands, saving the employee time and stress.

For SAS, a positive workplace goes beyond the company itself to include the entire ecosystem—from suppliers and partners to the institutional entities that influence the company's social and economic context. This is the spirit in which SAS was founded nearly thirty-five years ago, when it began as a collaboration between business and academia. The resulting initiatives and contributions have helped to build a culture of innovation in Italy, in particular by bolstering employment and by training recent graduates and talented youth.

"Being ranked among the first thirty-five companies in the Great Place to Work list confirms the success of the initiatives we have already undertaken and is a stimulus to continue in this direction," said Marco Icardi, SAS Italy Country Manager. "SAS never loses sight of the uniqueness of the individual or the national context, as we preserve at the country level the benefits and the guarantees of equality that have been established at the corporate level."[1]

Marco was frustrated. He was a forward-thinking employee working in a traditional hierarchical organization. Marco had asked his boss several times if he could take on additional tasks in his department, only to be told to concentrate on the narrow band of tasks he had been employed to do. He was criticized for showing

---

[1] At http://www.webwire.com/ViewPressRel.asp?aId=130126#.Uud5PoZAqIU, accessed January 2014.

initiative and going out of his way to assist a customer. Marco was told to follow the company's internal processes and to not deviate from them under any circumstances. After three months in his new job, he realized that there was little point putting in extra effort. His colleagues resented him and told him that he was showing everyone up by putting in extra effort. It make no difference to his pay, so he reluctantly dropped his standards. Marco was told not to talk to anyone in other departments unless he cleared it with his boss first. He got the distinct impression that his boss wanted total loyalty to him and no one else in the organization. Everyone around him came to work and believed that what they did was sheer drudgery. Some of the people in Marco's department had been there for over twenty-five years, and seemed to be favored when it came to rosters and leave claims. Junior staff were looked down on by managers. Training was competency-based and was focused exclusively on technical aspects of the job. While Marco appreciated the technical training, he wanted to grow and develop personally, but there was little opportunity to do so. When he asked his boss for some information about the company's plans over the next five years, he was told to "just do your job; if you need to know, I will tell you." Marco resigned in disgust and moved to greener pastures soon after. He was pleased to go and the company was pleased to see the back of him.

Marco found another job in what seemed to be a progressive-thinking company. He was immediately involved in a multi-skilling program. Marco was learning a variety of skills and capabilities. He enjoyed the variety and stimulation. Marco was encouraged to use his initiative with customers, and knew when and how to do so. The company had a performance bonus system in place, and this energized Marco to increase his personal productivity. While his last company was very bureaucratic and hierarchical, this company relied heavily on cross-functional teams centered on projects. Marco loved his new job. He found his work meaningful and rewarding;

he was engaged and committed. The company had flexible start and finish times and this allowed Marco to see his kids off to school in the morning. The company had a comprehensive learning and development program that covered many interesting topics such as financial management and personal development. Unlike his previous employer, Marco's new manager went to great lengths to inform him of the company's direction. Marco considers his new company an employer of choice.

This chapter introduces the New Employment Relationship Model. The model, based on sound research, takes into account the changing dynamics occurring from the workplace revolution discussed in the first three chapters. This revolution greatly changed the expectations employees and employers have of each other. The model serves as a benchmark for organizations wanting to gauge their culture around the eight shared values outlined in Chapter 1.

How is the model different to other HRD models?

There are several features that make the New Employment Relationship Model distinctive from other change models. One of its features is that it balances individual and organizational accountabilities for a set of shared values. The set of values supporting the model is diametrically opposite to the eight values of the old psychological contract illustrated in the Traditional Employment Relationship Model in Chapter 2. There are significant all-round benefits for meeting the new needs of employee and employer. Each value can be benchmarked. Other models, as I discussed in Chapter 3, neglect the changing dynamics in the employment relationship. They are more concerned with changing people's behavior than their thinking. These limitations are addressed in the New Employment Relationship Model.

A workplace's culture has a direct and indirect impact on organizational performance. Due to this realization, organizational culture has attracted considerable attention from researchers, organizational leaders, and consultants throughout the Western world. The New Employment Relationship Model assumes a collaborative partnership as distinct from a master/servant relationship like that supporting the old employment relationship. Dramatically altered expectations and a faster-moving and more uncertain environment have transformed organizations from stable and predictable to maneuverable and responsive structures. Concurrently, employees who have conventionally valued job security now need to build a portfolio of skills to retain employability. These fundamental shifts have not usually translated into accommodating workplace cultures. The model provides a roadmap for navigating the way forward, being mindful of the changing priorities of workers and bosses.

The distinctive characteristics of the model are that it is thorough, balanced, value-based, and practical. The model is one of the few empirically researched models of the psychological contract; it therefore has some rigor. It is based on a dual perspective of individual and organization. Most models are based on the needs of the organization, and either neglect the needs of the employee or assume that they will be accommodating to the organizational change. This model recognizes and considers both parties and their requirements. Rather than a process or tactic, the model is based on eight values. It is based on the assumption that people's beliefs are the genesis for their behavior. Most approaches are the reverse: they assume that by changing people's behavior, you ultimately change their beliefs. Instead of being theoretical, the model provides practical advice on how it can be applied in any workplace. These features of the New Employment Relationship Model set it apart from other change models.

This chapter gives a comprehensive overview of the model and its uniqueness. The subsequent eight chapters will take a closer look at each of the eight shared values.

What is the New Employment Relationship Model?

Table 4.1 illustrates the eight shared values and the appropriate responses from the perspectives of the individual and the organization.

Table 4.1   The New Employment Relationship Model

Shared value	Employee mindset	Employer mindset
Flexible deployment	*Willingness* to work in a variety of organizational roles and settings	*Encourage* employees to work in other organizational roles
Customer focus	*Serve* the customer before your manager	*Provide* information, skills, and incentives to focus externally
Performance focus	*Focus* on what you do, not where you work	*Link* rewards and benefits with performance rather than organizational dependency
Project-based work	*Accept* yourself as a project-based worker rather than a function-based employee	*Structure* work around projects rather than organizational functions
Human spirit and work	*Value* work that is meaningful	*Provide* work (wherever possible) that is meaningful
Commitment	*Commit* to helping the organization achieve its outcomes	*Commit* to helping employees to achieve their personal objectives
Learning and development	*Commit* to lifelong learning	*Enter* into a partnership for employee development
Open information	*Willing* to show enterprise and initiative	*Provide* employees with access to a wide range of information

I discussed my Traditional Employment Relationship Model in Chapter 2. For the sake of convenience and comparison, I have also included this model here, as Table 4.2.

Tables 4.1 and 4.2 list the polar benchmarks of the psychological contract. The similarities between the two are obvious. They are both based on eight shared values. Both describe the appropriate employee and employer mindsets for each corresponding values. The obvious difference is that the values are polar opposites and so are the associated employee and employer mindsets. Although I summarized the new values in Chapter 1, I think it would be helpful to briefly summarize here the old and new values in order to appreciate the juxtaposition of these two sets of values.

Table 4.2   The Traditional Employment Relationship Model

Shared value	Employee mindset	Employer mindset
Specialized employment	*Work* in a clearly defined and specialized employment area	*Offer* clearly defined and specialized employment opportunities
Internal focus	*Follow* organizational policies and practices	*Reinforce* the need to follow organizational policies and practices
Job focus	*Fulfill* job requirements	*Link* rewards and benefits to fulfilling job requirements
Functional-based work	*Focus* on job functions	*Structure* work around functions
Human dispirit and work	*Value* a stable and secure job	*Offer* stable and secure jobs
Loyalty	*Display* loyalty to the employer	*Reward* employees who are loyal to the organization
Training	*Commit* to gain technical qualifications	*Provide* opportunities for employees to develop technical skills
Closed information	*Comply* with managerial instructions	*Provide* sufficient information for employees to do their job

Specialized employment to flexible deployment

The value of specialized employment is concerned with offering clearly defined and specialized employment opportunities in exchange for a readiness to work in a clearly defined and specialized employment area. Conversely, flexible deployment is defined as encouraging employees to work in other organizational roles, in exchange for a willingness from employees to do so.

Internal focus to customer focus

Internal focus is essentially about reinforcing the need to follow organizational policies and procedures in exchange for willingness from employees to follow those policies and practices. Conversely, the value of customer focus is concerned with providing employees with the information, skills, and processes to focus on the needs of the customer, in exchange for employees serving the needs of customers wherever possible.

Job focus to performance focus

The value of job focus is linking benefits to fulfilling the requirements of the job in exchange for employees fulfilling those job requirements. Conversely, performance focus means linking rewards and benefits with performance instead of organizational dependency, in exchange for employees focusing on what needs to be done over where they work.

Functional-based work to project-based work

Functional-based work is structuring work around organizational functions in exchange for employees focusing on their job function. Conversely, project-based work is structuring work around projects rather than organizational functions in exchange for employees accepting that they are project-based workers rather than functional-based employees.

Human dispirit and work to human spirit and work

Human dispirit and work is based on the idea of offering stable and secure jobs in exchange for employees valuing stable and secure jobs. Conversely, human spirit and work is providing work, wherever possible, that is meaningful in exchange for employees valuing meaningful work opportunities.

Loyalty to commitment

Loyalty is concerned with rewarding employees who are loyal to the organization in exchange for employees displaying loyalty to their employer. Conversely, the value of commitment is about helping employees to achieve their personal objectives in exchange for their commitment to helping the organization achieve its objectives.

Training to learning and development

Training, in this sense, is concerned with providing opportunities for employees to develop their technical skills in exchange for commitment to gain technical qualifications. Conversely, learning and development is entering into a partnership for employee development in exchange for a commitment to be a lifelong learner.

Closed information to open information

Closed information means providing sufficient information for employees so that they are able to do their jobs and, in exchange, employees complying with managerial instructions. Conversely, open information means providing employees with access to a wide range of information in exchange for employees' willingness to show enterprise and initiative.

As you can see from these brief descriptions, the two sets of values in the models diametrically oppose each other. As such, they provide the two opposite ends of the continuum of the psychological contract. These yardsticks provide a way of monitoring progress for both entities in the employment relationship.

Who is responsible for making the New Employment Relationship Model work?

As I argued out in Chapter 2, any human relationship is based on an exchange between two people. In this context, the employment relationship is no different. The only difference between the old and new contract is what is offered by both parties and what they each expect in return from the other. All relationships that work are based upon shared responsibility.

In other words, both models are a mutual process of exchange with equal shared responsibility. This new partnership is formed jointly by fulfilling the requirements of both parties—the employee and employer. To satisfy the needs of both entities, there has to be an appreciation of the new requirements and a clear understanding of how they can be met in the context of the modern workplace. If managers fail to value the new needs of employees, they will not abide by their responsibilities. Equally, if traditional-thinking employees are unfamiliar with the new needs of a modern organization, they will not be able to fulfill their obligations. Both parties have a different set of accountabilities to make the new model work.

By way of an analogy, this individual/organization interface can be likened to the "yin and yang" relationship. In a yin/yang relationship, each half is incomplete and needs the other to achieve a unified whole. In the same way, the model specifies eight values to guide a new employer–employee partnership. In this way, there is a codependency between individual and organization. By codependency, I mean that the individual and organization are wholly reliant upon each other. The employee and employer were also codependent in the old employment relationship. In essence, the new employment codependency replaces the old codependency.

Managers and employees operating out from a conflicting mindset will be disappointed and frustrated about the signals they receive from the other partner in the relationship. For instance, an organizationally dependent employee is less likely to be flexible with customer requests, particularly if they interfere with company policy. The traditional-thinking employee, confusing an act of compliance with a gesture of organizational loyalty, will disappoint a customer-focused boss. Likewise, a modern-thinking worker will find that proactive behavior may be detrimental to his/her career in a bureaucratically-run organization. These misunderstandings, covered in earlier chapters, occur on a daily basis in most companies and violate trust and produce distress. Nevertheless, these paradigm shifts, and the inevitable tension they bring, provide an opportunity for companies to develop a new form of collaboration founded on an appreciation of the evolving individual and organizational way of thinking.

What is to be gained for both parties?

There are many benefits for both employee and employer in the new paradigm. Table 4.3 details these benefits with each value from the employee and employer perspective.

The individual benefits are linked to employability, development of new skills, greater job satisfaction, and more autonomy to make decisions. These advantages are consistent with the changing attitudes of employees outlined in Chapter 2. Therefore, employees who have these mindsets are likely to want to work in organizations that foster these values. The organizational benefits are greater flexibility, responsiveness, and maneuverability in the marketplace. These advantages are also consistent with the changing employer

Table 4.3   Benefits of the New Employment Relationship Model

Shared value	Benefit to employee	Benefits to employer
Flexible deployment	*Learn* a variety of skills and competencies to enhance employability within and outside the organization	*Enhance* maneuverability to respond faster to changing market forces
Customer focus	*Enhance* customer engagement skills to improve employability	*Retain* and *increase* market share
Performance focus	*Reward* for increased value to the organization	*Increase* productivity
Project-based work	*Develop* team-building skills and *add* variety and interest beyond functional role	*Improve* ability to respond quickly to challenges and opportunities in the marketplace
Human spirit and work	*Gain* greater satisfaction and meaning from work	*Retain* key staff and corporate knowledge
Commitment	*Build* career prospects	*Instill* greater commitment from employees to achieve organizational outcomes
Learning and development	*Broaden* the array of skills and competencies beyond the scope of current job	*Grow* and *develop* the organization
Open information	*Improve* capacity to make a greater organizational contribution	*Increase* responsiveness through quicker decision-making processes

needs listed in Chapter 2. Consequently, employers who promote these values are likely to attract and retain employees with a complementary mindset.

How is the new model applied?

Table 4.4 shows how to apply the eight values in a company. It illustrates the necessary strategies, key performance indicators (KPIs), and targets for developing a productive company culture based on the eight values.

Table 4.4   Application of the model

Shared value	Strategy	KPI	Target
Flexible deployment	*Implement* a coordinated multi-skilling program	*Develop* a skills matrix	*Assess* all employees in core competencies
Customer focus	*Coordinate* a comprehensive customer focus program	*Develop*, *implement*, and *analyze* annual customer satisfaction survey data	*Identify* improvements annually
Performance focus	*Replace job* descriptions with role descriptions	*Update* role descriptions for all employees	*Measure* performance against role descriptions
Project-based work	*Organize* work structures around projects	*Balance* functional and project-based tasks	*Involve* all employees in cross-functional teams
Human spirit and work	*Implement* a comprehensive employee engagement strategy	*Develop*, *implement*, and *analyze* annual employee engagement survey	*Identify* improvements annually
Commitment	*Develop* an enterprise agreement between employees and employer	*Monitor* the agreement	*Review* enterprise agreement annually
Learning and development	*Incorporate* personal development and problem-based learning into the HRD program	*Balance* expenditure in job skills, personal development, and problem-solving activities	*Review* expenditure annually
Open information	*Develop* a comprehensive information program	*Clarify* boundaries for enterprising employee behavior	*Observe* increase in appropriate employee initiative across the organization

The strategies are a combination of implementing programs, processes, engagements, applications, learning and development initiatives, and agreements. The successful use of these interventions cultivates the eight values in the organizational culture. Key performance indicators explain how these strategies will be monitored. These KPIs include internal and external annual surveys, performance appraisals, training program take-up, staff involvement in cross-functional activities and skill development, budgets, enterprise agreements, and up-to-date role descriptions. The targets are quantitative and qualitative standards to confirm the success or otherwise of the KPIs. Subsequent chapters will go into more detail on the use of each strategy.

As we all know, there is no shortage of HRD approaches designed to make organizations more flexible, customer-focused, performance-based, less functionally structured, to capture the "hearts and minds" of employees, obtain employee commitment, develop skills and competencies, and open information channels. But the use of these archetypal HRD tactics usually deals with a single area of change and overlooks the connection between workplace elements. For example, developing a change management strategy to engage employees in their work does not always consider how people's jobs are designed. But what someone does and how they are expected to go about doing it has an important bearing on their attitude to work. Or consider another example: strategies to make an organization more customer-focused may not factor in suitable rewards and recognition for superior service. All told, classic HRD strategies do not usually take a multidimensional perspective to change management. The result is, therefore, often disappointing.

Without a comprehensive approach, change management models are only partial solutions. The New Employment Relationship Model adopts a holistic approach to change. It recognizes that the psychological contract is complex and eclectic, including symmetry between the individual and the organization. Apart from appreciating a common set of values, the model recognizes the interdependencies between these values: each of the eight values impacts in some way on the other seven values.

We will discuss the eight shared values in depth in the following chapters, with each subsequent chapter being devoted to one of the eight values in the model. I have done this in the interest of clarity. A thorough understanding of the elements associated with each value will help you to assimilate the model and relate it to your organizational surroundings. Apart from giving you a practical understanding of each value, I offer some useful ways that the values can be integrated into your organization's culture. I have acknowledged that there are also numerous overlapping characteristics. For instance, the presence of the shared value of flexible deployment, with its emphasis on learning new skills and capabilities, is dependent on secondary elements of the related shared values of customer focus, performance focus, human spirit and work, commitment, learning and development, and open information. More specifically, customer service training—an element of customer focus—broadens and consequently enhances the skills of employees as a basis for greater flexibility.

The **10** Key Points …

1. The New Employment Relationship Model serves as a benchmark for organizations wanting to gauge their culture around the eight shared values.
2. The characteristics of the model are that it is thorough, balanced, value-based, and practical.
3. The old and new models of the employment relationship are the two opposite ends of the continuum of the psychological contract.
4. The new model is a mutual process of exchange with equal shared responsibility.

5   The individual benefits from the new model are linked to employability, the development of new skills, greater job satisfaction, and more autonomy to make decisions.

6   The organizational benefits from the new model are greater flexibility, responsiveness, and maneuverability in the marketplace.

7   The strategies for implementation of the new model are a combination of implementing programs, processes, engagements and applications, learning and development initiatives, and agreements.

8   Key performance indicators supporting the strategies of the new model include internal and external annual surveys, performance appraisals, training program take-up, staff involvement in cross-functional activities and skill development, budgets, enterprise agreements, and up-to-date role descriptions.

9   Conventional HRD strategies do not usually take a multidimensional perspective to change management. The result is often disappointing.

10 Without a comprehensive approach, change management models are only partial solutions. The New Employment Relationship Model adopts a holistic approach to change.

5
Learning and Earning
From specialist employment to flexible deployment

The adaptable employee is a product of and catalyst for the New Age economy.

Bill has been summoned to the HR manager's office from the production floor in the late afternoon. What have I done now? he thinks to himself. Bill takes the long stairway up to the manager's office, replaying the events of the day in his mind. Bill walks in and, after the usual pleasantries, takes a seat around the HR manager's conference table.

Kerry, the HR manager, gets straight to the point. "Bill, how would you like an increase in salary?" she begins.

Bill looks skeptically at Kerry without responding.

"As part of the latest workplace agreement, the company is about to embark on a course of job redesign for all employees in the production area. Multi-skilling will be the major emphasis of this job redesign. The goal is to enhance flexibility, efficiency, and job satisfaction," Kerry explains. "What are you forcing me to do?" Bill asks cautiously. "In keeping with employee wishes and with the national trend towards industrial democracy, this job redesign will be undertaken with the participation of all employees," Kerry replies. "You will not be forced to do any tasks you don't want to do. Managers will be responsible for leading the job redesign in their own departments.

They are to ensure that all employees have a fair input into the process, that Equal Employment Opportunity (EEO), health, safety, and welfare issues take top priority," Kerry continues. "Management believes that we can gain a net 3 percent in productivity gains. Measures of each department's success will include attendance rates, number of grievances registered, output, production costs, and other benchmark measures of efficiency and quality."

Bill asks, "What's in it for me?"

"You will have a greater variety of tasks to do and therefore will learn more skills and, we hope, have more job satisfaction; you will have a greater say in how your department operates; you will have better career opportunities; and, hopefully, you will have safer jobs. Depending on how the redesign takes shape, you will probably even have the opportunity to undertake complete projects and have more responsibility and decision-making in your jobs. And you will earn while you learn."

Kerry continues: "The company will benefit too. We will have a multi-skilled staff, improved occupational health and safety, improved and easier recruitment and retention due to increased levels of job satisfaction, more effective use of technology, improved staff morale …"

Bill interrupts. "It all sounds too good to be true! What's the catch?"

What does flexible deployment mean?

I define flexible deployment as the ability to transfer and apply skills and competencies across a range of tasks. Flexible deployment is essentially about utilizing an employee's skills and abilities in a range of roles and work situations. As we have discussed, it is more and more the case that, for employees to work effectively and efficiently, they need to learn and apply a wider range of skills. Although flexible work practices are increasingly common in the modern workplace, they are often not implemented properly, or for the right reasons. Done properly and for the right reasons, there are significant gains for both the employee and the employer.

A workplace that has a flexibly deployed workforce concentrates on three key things. Employees are trained and coached in areas beyond the scope of their regular job. This means learning new skills apart from their normal job function. Aligned with this training, a multi-skilling program is implemented across the organization. This means that the program should commence within departments first, and then spread across departments. In order to gain full buy-in from the workforce, incentives need to be put in place to encourage employees to learn new skills and capabilities. These three characteristics are critical for successfully and flexibly deploying the skills of employees across the organization.

In contrast, most traditional organizations that value specialist employment have no discernible link between their training and development program and flexible employment practices. Most training is done to reinforce current job skills and specialization. Employees are disadvantaged in their skill development in organizations operating from a traditional employment relationship mindset. More often than not in these organizations, if multi-skilling exists, it is used as a cost-cutting measure. The thinking behind this is: If we can train people to do a variety of tasks, we can reduce the number of employees and therefore cut our labor costs.

If the principal motive of managers in introducing flexible labor strategies is to reduce operating costs, then one of the costs that is usually minimized is labor. So, in these traditional organizational settings, the responsibility for up-skilling usually comes to rest squarely on the shoulders of the individual employee. Managers with a traditional cost-cutting attitude may seek to implement flexible deployment strategies as a way of minimizing the organization's training obligations and commitments towards employees. Although this is a widespread practice, the traditional cost minimization approach is not the right motive for implementing a flexible deployment policy.

Beginning any form of flexible work arrangement is largely dependent on the motives of management. Flexible forms of employment should not be used primarily as a cost-cutting strategy. Research suggests that, in many cases, flexible deployment of labor is synonymous with deregulation and the opportunity to cut employment costs. Enterprise flexibility does not necessarily mean deregulating the workforce. It certainly does not mean that the cost-cutting motive is appropriate in embarking on a strategy to become an employer of choice. Rather, it can—and should—be used as an important tool to fulfill the changing requirements of both employee and employer.

Why is flexible deployment important?

As we already know, the modern enterprise needs to be strategically adept, adaptable, and responsive in a rapidly evolving and increasingly competitive global marketplace. To be more maneuverable, a company needs to minimize hierarchy, and build a highly skilled workforce to engage in lifelong learning, problem-solving, and creative thinking. An enterprise that values the flexible deployment of employee skills and competencies has the capacity to break down job demarcations and boundaries around clearly defined functions within the business. This contributes to the agility of an organization. A flexibly deployed workforce offers managers a range of options for structuring and organizing employees to meet changing circumstances in their marketplace.

What's in it for employees?

A program that emphasizes multi-skilling beyond the scope of the current employees' capacity has several benefits for them. By learning a variety of new skills and competencies, employees obtain greater variety and more challenges in their work. For most employees, variety stimulates interest and potentially more enjoyment in their job. With more challenging work projects, employees can learn and grow on the job. Apart from the increased diversity and challenges, a multi-skilling program helps the individual to become a more skilled employee, and thus a more employable person. Being more employable means the employee is more valuable within and outside the organization.

There is a strong connection between adaptable employees and learning. Although employers cannot predict which employees will apply their new skill set, flexibility has consistently been associated with higher levels of cross-training. Individual workers with more capabilities are potentially better able to adjust to new situations, learn new tasks, and adopt new methods of performing old tasks. Companies that provide training tied to employees taking on multiple tasks are more likely to show larger gains in productivity than companies that follow traditional, more inflexible production methods. This is particularly the case when the training is coupled with wage incentives.

So, a properly implemented flexible employment program is in the interests of the organization and the individual employee. A flexible deployment program stresses the need for flexible forms of organizing work, in ways that fulfill both the wishes of employees and the requirements of external competition.

To create a learning organization, managers need to place a high degree of trust in staff, and have a strong adherence to the shared value of flexible deployment. What is more, the flexible deployment of employee skills needs to be backed up by sound systems of communication, participation, and involvement. Investment in time and money needs to remain high for a considerable period of time. This focus needs long-term commitment from everybody. It is nonetheless worth the time and effort: flexible deployment work practices go a long way to meeting the criteria for an employer of choice. Employees in a company characterized as an employer of choice have a greater degree of self-sufficiency.

Above all, a multi-skilled workplace enables an organization to be more responsive in a global economy. When rapid change occurs in the marketplace, a company needs to respond with speed and agility. The most innovative organizations are those that are likely to have workforces that are flexibly applying a wide range of skills to the work challenges at hand. Employers of choice are firms that cultivate a culture of learning. Employees in these high-performing firms are encouraged to exchange information and skill sets. Knowledge and information create flexibility in the way work can be carried out. Flexible deployment can lead to improved product lines, production processes, and marketing strategies, all with the same workforce.

At the same time, flexible deployment is also a critical requirement of the modern employee. The information economy places a premium on the worker's ability to move from a job in one workplace to another with minimal adjustment. The need for mobility means the ability to learn new jobs in the same company, to do several different types of tasks in the same day, or to adjust quickly to several different kinds of employment cultures and different group situations.

There is considerable incentive for progressive employees to move beyond the old functional employment model that promotes specialization, to develop and expand their employee skill base. Apart from being more successful in navigating a fast-moving marketplace, companies that promote and reward multi-skilled staff will continue to attract these enlightened employees. The old mindset characteristic of the past century was to promote people who were specialists in their field. For instance, most managers are still promoted to management because they have great technical skills, rather than demonstrating an aptitude to be a leader. On the other hand, today's new mindset is to reward employees who deploy their skills beyond their functional specialization. For instance, people with a wide array of skills may be given challenging projects to complete. The adaptable employee is a product of the New Age economy. Forward-thinking employees are expected to learn new work processes, to shift jobs several times in the course of a career, to move geographically and, if necessary, to learn entirely new vocations. Employees with these aptitudes are sought after in the current climate.

Why is specialization being replaced by flexible deployment?

As a member of the baby boomer generation, when I left school my parents encouraged me to find a specialization as a means of gaining job security. Their thinking went something like this: If you can find a niche where you could use specialized skills, you could define a market segment for yourself. But this line of thinking was based on a stable and predictable marketplace. The logic no longer applies; the rules have changed.

Here are two practical illustrations of this.

Being an optometrist was considered a safe specialization when I left school. Do several years of study, and you will have a secure job for life. After all, the reasoning was that most people will wear spectacles at some point. But with the advent of optical laser surgery, more and more people are opting for this method instead of buying prescription glasses. Of course there is still a healthy market for glasses, but it is a shrinking market. Optometrists now need to supplement their profession by diversifying into selling sunglasses, which is an expanding market.

In the trades, there are also many examples of traditionally secure jobs that are now being challenged. For example, hardware stores are now teaching people basic skills in renovating their homes. Many of these tasks were once done by carpenters, builders, and landscape gardeners. Now people are learning home renovation skills thanks to these DIY courses. So it is risky for individuals to put all their eggs in one basket and narrow their job focus to a single specialty. A far more effective approach is to create the scope and flexibility to deploy their skills in a variety of settings and work areas.

What are the strategies of flexible deployment?

The most common strategies of flexible deployment are job rotation, job enrichment, job enlargement, and multi-skilling. In this section, I will briefly define each of these and give examples of how organizations have successfully implemented these approaches.

Job rotation

Job rotation is an approach where an individual is moved through a schedule of organizational projects designed to give him or her breadth of exposure to the entire operation. It is also carried out to allow qualified employees to gain more insight into the processes of a company, and to reduce boredom and increase job satisfaction through variety. The term "job rotation" can also mean the scheduled exchange of persons in regional or international offices. At senior management levels, job rotation—frequently referred to as management rotation—is tightly linked with succession planning; that is, developing a pool of people capable of stepping into an existing job. Here the goal is to provide learning experiences that facilitate changes in thinking and perspective.

If an employee is looking for a career move that offers new roles, responsibilities, and skills, job rotation can accommodate that need within the employee's current company. As Woody Allen (as Alvy Singer) said to Diane Keaton (as Annie) in the 1976 movie *Annie Hall*: "A relationship ... is like a shark. It has to constantly move forward or it dies. And I think what we've got on our hands is a dead shark."[1] If an employee is feeling like a dead shark in their current position, they need look no further than their current organization to get swimming again. This, of course, assumes that the organization embraces job rotation as a flexible deployment strategy.

Generally speaking, the employees I speak to who are involved in job rotation comment that they stay more challenged, feel a greater sense of fulfillment, and develop a greater sense of obligation to their current organization. Managers I have spoken to who have adopted job rotation as a strategy say it has increased both staff retention and effectiveness.

For example, FedEx, a multinational logistics services corporation based in the United States, have a successful job rotation program in place. Detailed preparation helps to minimize the risks involved in switching jobs at FedEx. Such pre-rotation collaboration is part of what makes the program work. The employees who are swapping jobs work together to discuss how to transition the work. It makes sense for this to be done at the employee level. It creates a partnership between the individuals to ensure the rotation is successful. Detailed preparation helps to minimize the risks associated with switching jobs. The biggest concern for FedEx in the implementation of their job rotation program is that customers

---

[1] At http://www.youtube.com/watch?v=6RFH9_M0OaY, accessed January 2014.

are not adversely affected. During the six-month rotation, the two employees swapping would effectively have two jobs. That is to say, they would retain responsibilities for their original position as well as taking on the duties of the new one. Both employees agree in advance to own each other's projects, but the original leader would handle personnel issues. This ensures that nothing falls between the cracks, and eases any employee concerns about the switch.

Job enrichment

Job enrichment is a way to motivate employees by giving them increased responsibility and variety in their jobs. Many traditional employers believed that money is the only true motivating factor for employees and that if you want to get more productivity out of employees, offering them more money is the only way to do it. While that may be true for some people, the majority of workers today enjoy stimulating work and want to be appreciated for the work they do. Job enrichment—allowing employees to have more control in planning their work and deciding how the work should be accomplished—is one way to tap into the natural desire of most employees to do a good job, to be appreciated for their contributions to the company, and to feel more a part of the team.

The strategy of job enrichment has its foundations in Frederick Herzberg's *two-factor theory*. According to Herzberg, two separate dimensions contribute to an employee's behavior at work. The first dimension, which he referred to as "hygiene factors," involves the presence or absence of things that are potential demotivators, such as wages, working environment, rules and regulations, and supervisors. When these factors are perceived to be poor, work is dissatisfying and employees are not motivated. However, according to Herzberg, having positive hygiene factors does not necessarily make employees motivated: it simply keeps them from being dissatisfied. The second dimension of Herzberg's theory refers to "motivators," which are factors that satisfy higher-level needs such as recognition for doing a good job, achievement, and the opportunity for growth and responsibility. These motivators are what actually increase job satisfaction and performance. Job enrichment becomes an important strategy at this point because enriching employees' jobs can help meet some of their motivational needs. There are five areas that are believed to affect employee motivation and job performance. These are:

- skill variety
- task identity
- task significance
- autonomy, and
- feedback.

Job enrichment seeks to find positive ways to address each of these areas and so improve employee motivation and personal satisfaction.

Skill variety involves the number of different types of competencies that are used to do a job. *Task identity* is a matter of realizing a visible outcome from performing a task. Being able to see the end result of their work is an important motivator for employees. *Task significance* involves how important the task is to others in the company, which is significant for showing employees how their work fits in with that done in the rest of the organization. *Autonomy* involves the degree of freedom, independence, and decision-making ability of employees in completing assigned tasks. *Feedback* describes how much and what type of information about job performance employees receive.

Considering these five components, there are many different types of job enrichment activities and programs that companies can implement to encourage employee participation and enhance their motivation. At any rate, the purpose of job enrichment is to improve the quality of an employee's job and therefore motivate the employee to accomplish more.

The job enrichment concept was developed based on an experiment carried out by the Swedish car manufacturer Volvo in the 1960s. Volvo's management decided to try discontinuing one of its assembly lines and instead putting all the people with the skills needed in the assembly line in one room with all the tools and equipment needed to carry out the operations. The length of the car-building process increased, and hence so did the costs. However, the overall life cycle cost of the car product, including all the required repair work, guarantee work, clients' dissatisfaction factors, and so on, decreased significantly. Taken as a whole, there was an improvement in quality and a reduction in costs.

Based on the results of this experiment, Volvo was the first car manufacturer to introduce job enrichment as a form of flexible deployment in their organizational design. It was decided that the increased opportunities for enriching creative work increased the level of responsibility and ownership. Increasing the line of sight between employees' work and the final product enhanced motivation and therefore increased employees' ability to perform good work and check for quality. It was decided at Volvo—and, subsequently many other companies—that, in order to increase people's productivity, it is critical to give them more opportunities for independent and creative work.

Job enlargement

Job enlargement refers to increasing the scope of a job by extending its range of duties and responsibilities. This approach is the antithesis of specialization and the division of labor. Specialist employment practices organize work into smaller, clearly defined units, each of which is performed repetitively by an individual worker. The boredom and alienation caused by job specialization can actually cause efficiency to fall, so job enlargement seeks to reverse the process of specialization and create an environment where employees find their work more meaningful.

There is a difference between job enrichment and job enlargement. Job enrichment means improvement, or an increase with the help of upgrading and development, whereas job enlargement means adding more duties, and an increased workload. In job enrichment, an employee finds satisfaction in the personal growth potential, while job enlargement refers to having duties and responsibilities that are additional to their current role description.

A typical approach might be to replace assembly lines with modular work: Instead of an employee repeating the same step on each product, they perform several tasks on a single item. To enlarge the job, employees need to be retrained in new fields. This can take time. Results have shown that the positive effects of job enlargement can diminish after a period of time. In other words, even the enlarged job role becomes mundane. This in turn can lead to similar levels of demotivation and job dissatisfaction at the expense of increased training levels and costs. The continual enlargement of a job over time is also known as "job creep," which can lead to an unmanageable workload.

Multi-skilling

Multi-skilling is a coordinated approach to train or coach individuals to undertake a variety of work tasks within the same organization, although multi-skilling is not the same as being a generalist. A multi-skilled employee is expected to be competent in more than one function and might be described as a versatile specialist. The challenge is to combine flexibility with a set of core competencies. A successful multi-skilling program must deal with four issues:

- the skills identified
- the training required
- how work will be covered, and
- how and when the work will be executed.

Multi-skilling can be developed through a variety of techniques:

- coaching and mentoring
- job rotation (secondments and exchanges)
- job shadowing
- learning by doing
- self-learning
- temping, and
- team-based cross-functional projects.

Most people need to update their knowledge at least every five years to stay current. To ensure this happens, it is helpful to have a structured and comprehensive approach to learning skills on the job. Ensuring that all employees have opportunities from time to time to work on cross-functional projects is also helpful in broadening vision, understandings, and skills. To further encourage multi-skilling, it is helpful to ensure that appraisal and reward systems also reflect the importance of this strategy.

Specialist skills remain central to organizational and career success. But, as the nature of work alters, the importance of functional flexibility is growing. Managers have a role to support and facilitate this process with their staff.

AT THE COALFACE

United Kingdom food producer Campbell's Grocery Products wanted to make the most of their technicians' skills using the flexible deployment strategy of multi-skilling. The company recognized that its twenty technicians—10 percent of the total workforce—were underused. Their role was to work on the production line, helping operators, and come off the line to repair breakdowns. But their on-line duties prevented them from practicing their skills. All twenty technicians were subsequently trained in both electrical and mechanical skills to attain a multi-skilled standard required. This was done over two and half years. Most of the training was delivered internally, on site, during each technician's shift. The results were quantifiable: stock accuracy improved, the number of breakdowns reduced, customer response times shortened, and the time taken to repair faults decreased. Simultaneously, technicians' morale and team spirit greatly improved, especially as a result of the increased efficiencies generated by the training, which resulted in less "firefighting" and frustration. The technicians' former feelings of irritation were replaced by feeling that they are contributing to the site's success.[2]

---

[2] No author cited (2007) "Campbell's makes double of its technicians' skills: Win–win achieved for employees and company." *Human Resource Management International Digest* 15(1), 20–22.

How do you start the process of multi-skilling?

The best way to start is to create a skills matrix. The first practical step to implant the value of flexible deployment in an organization's culture is to apply a coordinated multi-skilling and retraining program for all staff. This program should initially start within each team, department, or function. Once entrenched in each business unit, a cross-departmental or cross-functional program should follow. That is to say, before looking at cross-functional flexible deployment across the organization, all employees should be exposed to a variety of skills within their departmental area. After demonstrating their mastery of several skills, tasks, or competencies within their functional area, employees can then embark on acquiring skills in other departments.

Not all tasks need to be open to multi-skilling. In large enterprises, this would be impractical anyway. Nevertheless, wherever possible, an attempt should be made to ensure that more than one—and possibly several—employees can perform each organizational role or task to a minimum required standard. The more multi-skilled employees are, the more flexible the organization is in terms of staff deployment, and the more skilled the workforce. This is commonly referred to as a win–win situation. Or, if you consider the consumer as well, you might refer to this as a win–win–win situation.

To coordinate and monitor this process, each department within the company should develop and adopt a skills matrix. A skills matrix can be defined as the breakdown and recording of all the tasks necessary for the department to function effectively and achieve its objectives. All employees are then assessed against these tasks in terms of their degree of competency. The first step in this process is to identify the range of tasks, roles, or competencies required within that particular department or section of the business. Once this has been defined and established, the second step is to assess the skill level of each employee to do these tasks. Step three is to coordinate a learning program for all staff so they can become multi-skilled beyond their immediate role.

The old adage is true: What gets rewarded gets done. To supplement this multi-skilling process, and to encourage a flexible learning environment, each employee ought to receive some form of incentive to learn a predetermined number of skills, beyond the scope of their current role. Table 5.1 shows what the skills matrix could look like.

Six employees are shown in the skills matrix within a specific function of a business. For instance, this could be the marketing, accounts, or human resources departments. Numbers 1 to 9 along the top of the matrix illustrate that there are nine core tasks, roles, or competencies required within that department or section of the business. White

Table 5.1   Skills matrix

Staff member/Competency	1	2	3	4	5	6	7	8	9
Joe	Undergoing	Trainer	Trainer	Trainer	Competent				
Mary	Competent	Undergoing	Undergoing	Undergoing	Trainer	Trainer	Competent	Undergoing	Undergoing
Bill			Undergoing	Undergoing	Trainer	Trainer	Trainer		
Harry			Undergoing	Competent					
Sue			Undergoing						
Kathy	Trainer		Undergoing					Trainer	

Legend

Trainer	
Competent	
Undergoing training	
Not yet trained	

spaces on the matrix, signifying "Not yet trained," represent competencies that require training for that particular staff member. For instance, Joe requires training in competencies 6, 7, 8, and 9. In other words, this skills matrix indicates that Joe has had no exposure in the form of training or coaching in these organizational tasks.

Light grey spaces on the matrix ("Undergoing training") represent competencies where the individual has had some training or coaching, but has not yet achieved a consistent minimum acceptable standard of performance without close supervision, coaching, or training. For example, Joe has commenced training in competency 1 in the table, but has not achieved proficiency.

Dark grey spaces ("Competent") represent tasks in which the individual has achieved competency. For example, Joe has achieved mastery in competency 5, as shown in the above table. Competency in this case can be defined as having achieved a consistent minimum acceptable standard of performance on the job and so the employee is able to complete that task in an unsupervised capacity.

Black spaces ("Trainer") identify individuals who have achieved competency and have been delegated the task of training or coaching their fellow employees in that skill area. For example, Joe is qualified to train or coach his fellow team members in competencies 2, 3, and 4. To qualify as a workplace trainer, that individual must have certain qualifications and attributes. They must have reasonably good communication skills, have achieved and demonstrated competency in that skill area, and completed a foundation "train the trainer"' program.

As I mentioned earlier, a rewards and incentives program should be linked to this skills matrix. Using the above example, Mary is the most multi-skilled of the six employees within the department. She has achieved a minimum acceptable standard of performance in five task areas. So, from a skills acquisition point of view, she is currently the most valuable—and, arguably, most crucial—member of the team, unit, or department. She therefore qualifies for some form of reward or incentive for learning and applying these new skills. Joe, Bill, and Kathy are the only employees in that department, apart from Mary, who have qualified to train or coach their colleagues. They should all be rewarded for this level of proficiency too.

Once all the departments or functional areas within an organization have a flexibly deployed workforce, the next step is to create a skills matrix that is cross-functional. A new skills matrix can then be developed and adopted across functional boundaries and include cross-functional competencies. The objective in the first instance is to generate multi-skilling within each functional area of the business.

What are the benefits of a skills matrix?

The benefit for the employee of accumulating a broad range of competencies is becoming more employable within and beyond their current organization. For the business, the benefit is a more responsive organization that is able to respond to the ever-changing demands of the marketplace.

Specifically, the skills matrix serves four important purposes:

- It provides an up-to-date visual representation of the status of skill development for a group of employees.
- It assists both managers and staff to plan skills development for the future. For instance, on competency 1 in the above example, it is clear that Kathy could plan to commence training with Sue, Harry, and Bill. She could also complete Joe's training. On the other hand, Bill, being qualified to train in competencies 5, 6, and 7, can plan to commence training with Harry, Sue, and Kathy.
- With the connection between incentives and skills development, the matrix can add some degree of objectivity to the decision of who is rewarded for acquiring new skills.
- It can be used to strategically plan training for new and existing staff. New competencies can be added to the matrix as the business grows or changes direction. This maintains the currency of the matrix and is an up-to-date reflection of the functional skills required and the status of skill levels within that part of the company.

To be consistent, it is important that one person (usually the manager) assesses the skill level and is the only one responsible for changing the status of the skills matrix. For example, if the manager has observed a staff member on several occasions carry out a task or competency to a minimum standard of performance, s/he can record this on the matrix. This encourages managers to specify their standards of performance and communicate them to staff members. It also requires the manager to be objective in his/her assessment of staff. In terms of targets, the ideal would be for all staff to be assessed as competent in all areas of the business by a set date. This date can be negotiated between the manager and his/her staff.

In summary, and referring back to the New Employment Relationship Model in Chapter 4, the appropriate individual response to the value of flexible deployment is a willingness to work in a variety of organizational roles and settings. To demonstrate this new mindset, the individual needs to show he is prepared to take on new tasks, be open to incentives to learn new skills, competencies, and tasks, and be prepared to learn quickly. The appropriate organizational response is to encourage employees to work in other organizational roles. To be able to do this, the organization needs to increase the task responsibilities of employees using any of the job design strategies outlined in this chapter, and put in place incentives for skills attainment. These mindsets and the appropriate responses from both entities in the employment relationship will go a long way towards shifting from a value of specialized employment to flexible deployment.

The **10** Key Points ...

1. Flexible deployment is the ability to transfer and apply skills and competencies across a range of tasks.

2. The benefit of this for the organization is that a flexibly deployed workforce is strategically adept, adaptable, and responsive in a fast-paced and hyper-competitive global marketplace.

3. The benefit of this for the employee is that, by being more skilled, they are more valuable within and outside the organization and therefore more employable.

4. The most common strategies for flexible deployment are job rotation, job enrichment, job enlargement, and multi-skilling.

5. A successful multi-skilling program must deal with four issues: the skills identified; the training required; how work will be covered; and how and when the work will be executed.

6. The best way to start a multi-skilling program is to create a skills matrix.

7. Once all departments have a flexibly deployed workforce, the next step is to create a cross-functional skills matrix.

8. The benefit of a skills matrix for the employee is the opportunity to accumulate a broad range of competencies.

9. The benefit of a skills matrix for the employer is a more responsive organization that is able to respond to the ever-changing demands of the marketplace.

10. The appropriate individual response to the value of flexible deployment is a willingness to work in a variety of organizational roles and settings, and the appropriate organizational response is to encourage employees to work in other organizational roles.

6

Customer-centricity

From internal focus to customer focus

Being clear about who your customer is, and spending time providing a value-added service is a much less energy-draining and more personally affirming use of an employee's time than wallowing in the internal ambiguity of a dying bureaucracy.

Mary was becoming increasingly frustrated. Her bank decided to stop a special arrangement she had had with her previous bank manager. This arrangement allowed Mary to undertake certain transactions expeditiously. This arrangement was different to the normal bank policy. Due to the bank lacking a system to record such an arrangement, the new staff member refused to honor Mary's previous arrangement with her bank manager.

When the new staff member refused to process Mary's request, she asked to speak to the branch manager. The staff member chose to speak to a supervisor instead. The supervisor also said no, claiming it was against bank policy. This was despite Mary's assurances that she had an arrangement in place.

More and more aggravated, Mary demanded the branch manager's name and email address. After some discussion, she was eventually given those details.

Mary subsequently fired off an email to the branch manager explaining the problem, requesting re-confirmation of the previous arrangement and a method of recording the decision. The email also requested the name and email address of a higher-level manager should the branch manager choose to refuse her request.

To Mary's surprise, a relief branch manager responded, as the regular branch manager was on vacation. His response did not address Mary's concerns, and again stated the standard bank policy. Further, the relief branch manager responded by giving Mary the standard free number for the customer relations department and a website address to lodge the complaint.

Even more frustrated, Mary requested the details of the manager of the customer relations department. Having emailed them, the manager called Mary. However, Mary was in a meeting and so the manager left her a message. Mary called back at the conclusion of her meeting and was told by a recorded message that she had called outside standard business hours, which were between 9:30 a.m. and 4:30 p.m. Mary had called at 4:40 p.m.

Mary's frustration turned to anger. She again requested the contact details of someone interested in her feedback. The Head of Customer Relations finally called Mary back. They had an extensive discussion, but she was unable or unwilling to change the bank's position. However, she did give Mary the name and contact details for the area manager.

Mary called the area manager and they had a discussion about her situation. He still wasn't willing to allow Mary to have her own way. However, the area manager was concerned that Mary had been unable to speak directly with her bank manager, and he promised to put a note on the file for Mary's unusual transaction.

The branch manager returned from vacation. Mary rang the call center again; she couldn't get through to the branch. The branch manager rang back on Monday, but missed Mary, leaving his number. Mary called back, and the call went straight to the branch (hooray!).

It took two minutes for Mary to discuss the issue with her bank manager and for him to reinstate her arrangement. To complete the transaction, Mary went to another branch. She stated that she had a special arrangement with the branch, the teller looked it up, found the details, and successfully processed Mary's transaction.

More than ever, everything a manager thinks, says, and does should directly or indirectly focus on the needs and wishes of the company's customers. Most customers today are more demanding than in the past, and their options for taking their business elsewhere are better than ever before in a deregulated global economy. Poor responsiveness to the demands and requests of the customer will today, more than ever, adversely affect a business's market share. Then again, companies that position and focus their resources and skills on dealing with customers are likely to gain additional customers and sustain their viability. The customer is king may be a cliché but it is nonetheless very true, and likely to continue to be so for the foreseeable future.

Over the past thirty or so years, the emphasis has shifted from a value of internal focus to a value of customer focus. Conventional thinking suggested that, by having efficient processes and practices in place internally, organizations were likely to meet a reasonably clearly and consistently defined array of requests from their customer base. This internal focus on efficiency and consistency made good sense in a reasonably predictable marketplace.

employees have to juggle the often competing needs of the company and the wants of the customer.

Now an increasingly unpredictable marketplace has shifted the emphasis to a focus on the customer's priorities first and foremost. Competition has heightened, and customers' demands have become more challenging and their needs more diverse. Being able to put internal processes and procedures in place to meet this greater variation in customer demands is no longer a viable proposition. A new way is needed. This new approach means those employees who deal directly with customers must be problem solvers who go beyond simple adherence to organization policies and processes. They now have to juggle the often competing needs of the company and the wants of the customer.

Sales and marketing personnel are more than ever the "meat in the sandwich" between these two entities—the organization and the customer. This conflict requires employees to develop new skills in problem solving, lateral thinking, and innovation. It follows that it is in employees' best interests to develop these skills in the new economy. Both the company and employees should value a customer-focused approach rather than an internally-focused approach.

In response to this juggling act, managers ought to invest more resources in identifying and dealing with a wider array of customer demands. Employees too must be willing to change their mindset and learn when and how to display initiative and enterprise. So it is in the interest of both employee and employer to adopt a customer-focused mindset.

How is customer focus different from customer service?

The concept of customer focus is different from customer service. In a nutshell, customer focus is about focus: everything—whether thought or action—has the interests of the customer in mind. Customer service, on the other hand, is the provision of quality service to their customer base within the confines of their company's policies and procedures. Despite the fact that the concept of customer focus has been around since the beginning of industry, organizational leaders are still challenged by putting into practice strategies that will assist in increasing and maintaining the spotlight on the needs and interests of the customer. It is one of those perennial challenges facing enterprises.

In this regard, three key issues still require the attention of managers: valid, reliable, and fair reward systems for exemplary customer-focused behavior; the development of new skills to deal with the customer interface; and restrictive career paths for customer workers. These issues have been the stumbling block to enhancing and maintaining focus on the customer.

More specifically, clear and understood roles for employees who work directly with customers help them to develop confidence and avoid the inevitable conflict between the often competing demands of the customer and the company. In concert with this is a requirement for a consistent, fair, and valid incentives system for desirable customer-focused behavior. A comprehensive, well implemented, and used Customer Relationship Management (CRM) system is critical. Customer relationship management balances technical and human customer service requirements. Also, all staff are likely to benefit from tailored, timely, and relevant customer service training and development opportunities.

Three additional elements are implicit in developing a customer-focused culture within an organization: an effective internal customer service climate, adequate resources to support the customer interface, and committed leadership from management to implement these fundamentals. These elements combine to facilitate a customer-focused company culture, and require energy and input from both individual and organization.

What exactly is customer focus?

At its most basic level, customer focus captures the relationship between an employee of a company and the customer of an organization after a sale has been made or a service has been rendered. Customer service representatives are brokers between the organization and its customers. In this boundary-spanning role, people who work directly with customers are the agents who negotiate between organizational needs and customer expectations. The range of employees involved in customer work is expanding. For instance, sales work involves a component of customer work. Salespersons promoting a firm's products or services increasingly have to meet customers' needs long after the sale has been completed; for example, in the insurance industry, long-term relationships can be common practice.

The perpetual challenges of implementing customer-focused organizational structures, processes, and systems are more confronting now than ever before in a climate of intense competition and heightened customer expectations. This interface between the customer and organization continues to pose special problems for both organizations and employees. These challenges are magnified by the pressure to be responsive to the problems a company's customer is trying to solve. Yet implementing organizational structures, processes, and systems that facilitate a focus on customers is still problematic in most industries. This is partly attributable to the relative paucity of information in the popular management literature on the strategic organizational changes required to achieve this customer-focus objective. Also, there is not enough empirical research on implementing these changes. The majority of books on this subject are more concerned with how employees should interact with the customer. Little is said about the "big picture": how organizational leaders create support processes to manage the relationship between the organization and the customer.

What are these "big picture" challenges?

From my observations, there are three challenges that are rarely discussed in books on the subject. First: How do you reward someone fairly and consistently for great customer-focused behavior? How do you ensure that the reward system is suitable and dependable? Just knowing where to begin is difficult enough. For instance, should employees be rewarded for following customer service processes or for accomplishing great outcomes? It is easy to argue for either way, but then how do companies ensure that the value of the reward is commensurate with the deed? Then you have the implementation issues of rewards: where and when to start, and how often and how much? On the other hand, by not recognizing exemplary customer-focused behavior, managers send a clear signal to employees that the company is not that serious about being customer focused. By the way, one of the simplest, most effective, and often neglected ways of rewarding exemplary behavior is to dedicate time at meetings to recognize this work publicly in all its forms. If meeting time is regularly devoted to acknowledge commendable customer work, the organization is not only recognizing and reinforcing this behavior, it is also showing its importance. Although this simple form of recognition doesn't answer the questions around consistency and reliability, it is a good starting point.

A second challenge is the development of new skills to deal with any out-of-the-ordinary demands by customers. Anyone managing long-term relationships with major customer accounts would know that it requires skills well beyond personal selling and negotiation. The qualities needed are many and varied. To be customer focused, in a practical sense, requires an emphasis on teamwork, a breadth of experience, empathy, an understanding and appreciation of the goals and constraints on people in other functional areas of the business, and flexibility in being able to react to changing business conditions. These are only a few of the traits needed. Sending people off to generic customer service training programs is not the whole answer. Formal customer service training programs ought to be supplemented with mentoring, coaching, problem solving, and increased understanding of business activities. These activities are not one-offs; they require continuous attention.

The third challenge is limited career paths. Traditionally, there is no defined career path for people who choose to work in the customer service area of a business. Vertical progression for sales and marketing personnel is comparatively limited. Moreover, the prevailing wisdom is that, to advance to general management, employees need experience in a variety of functional areas. The upshot of career limitations in customer service roles means that good people with ambition move on and leave when they are offered other opportunities. The customer is left in the lurch. Retaining good staff at the customer interface then becomes an issue. The answer to this predicament is to ensure that some of the strategies of flexible deployment discussed in the previous chapter are applied within the sales and marketing departments.

These three issues in particular need to be adequately addressed if an organization wants to develop a customer-focused culture.

From the employee perspective, these structural changes can be just as demanding. One of the fundamental difficulties of implementing customer-focused strategies is an acceptance by those working with customers of a new way of working. For instance, sophisticated technological CRM systems can isolate people who naturally enjoy social interaction. Customer service employees often resist these new technological changes in work practices because of the threat of social separation that information technology systems can bring.

Also, there can be significant resistance to internally sharing customer-based information. This is particularly the case when organizational reward systems don't value information sharing. For instance, a well-known international commercial retail travel agency I consulted with was concerned with what it perceived to be a lack of teamwork among their travel agents in the retail outlets. They wanted me to "fix" the problem. I asked the managing director how he rewarded his staff. He told me that at the end of each month a table was published with each agent's name and the value of sales they had made during the month. Bonuses were paid on the basis of these figures. "Can you see the problem with this bonus system?" I asked. So determined were these employees to improve their sales figures, they would not share information within the office. Once he had accepted this, this managing director cited an example of a salesperson "stealing" a lead from a colleague's desk while they were out to lunch. The salesperson decided to call the customer and book the flight for them in their colleague's absence. Not mentioning this to their colleague, the person who had "taken the initiative" was credited with the sale. The individually-based reward system works against teamwork in this instance.

As I mentioned earlier, employees in customer service areas often have less scope for moving up the organization than their colleagues. This can be a demotivator for ambitious and capable employees who want to progress. Their alternative is to look for another job in another company in an entirely different area. Turnover in customer-related roles is often relatively high, and a contributing factor is likely to be minimal scope for vertical progression.

While it is easy and well accepted to say that modern companies should be more customer focused, there are many different interpretations of what it means to be customer focused and little understanding and appreciation of the magnitude of the challenges ahead. As challenging as it is for employees and organizational leaders, the paradigm shift from internal to customer focus has never been more important than it is now. In some cases, a dramatic change in thinking is required. This can mean a shift from a process-driven, quality-controlled internal business environment to one that sees itself as a business entity existing and revolving around its customers' orbit. A failure to make this shift from internal to customer focus is likely to result in those companies being left behind by their competitors who have overcome this dilemma.

Which elements are needed to develop a customer-focused culture?

Like all eight values in the model, promoting the value of customer focus is a successful interchange between employer and employee. There are four important elements to creating a customer-focused culture:

- clear and understood customer workers' roles, responsibilities, and priorities;
- consistent, fair, and valid incentives for customer-focused behavior;
- a comprehensive, well implemented, and utilized CRM system; and
- tailored, timely, and relevant customer service training opportunities.

Even with the obvious overlap, we will look at each element separately and consider some practical advice for their successful implementation and adoption.

Role clarity

The boundary-spanning nature of the customer worker's role provides unique challenges. Because of this distinct position in a brokerage role between the organization and customer, people in customer service roles are open to experiencing conflict in their role. This is because employees working directly with customers have to deal with competing demands from the organization and the customer on a regular basis. Any work associated with the interaction between a company and its customers can potentially generate some role conflict. This possible conflict can cause grief for the employee, his/her customer, and the associated company.

This is because any work with a customer places employees in the unique position of answering to two bosses: the organization and the customer. Although not formally designated as a boss, the customer nonetheless represents an additional set of interests and demands to which the customer service employee has to respond. Role conflict can potentially play out in a variety of ways. For example, consider a situation in which a customer service officer is asked by a loyal customer to provide technical support for a product that is not covered by the customer's purchase contract with the company. As we have all experienced as customers, this can be—and often is—turned down by the company. These requests are more often than not viewed as an inappropriate use of the organization's time and resources. This often causes conflict between the customer service officer and the customer. In this example, the customer service officer may turn down the request. In doing so, the employee fails to meet the requirements of the customer. They are acting in the interests of the organization. On other occasions the customer service officer may be inclined to cut a few corners to satisfy the customer. While the customer is likely to be happy in these circumstances, the boss of the customer service department may react negatively. Either way, the customer service officer is likely to experience conflict, either from the customer or their manager. The boundary-spanning nature of the role is likely to regularly place employees, who work with customers, in these kinds of predicaments. If success is defined in terms of meeting both the company's and the customer's expectations, then both employees in this situation have failed!

In this scenario, the first employee is internally focused; that is, has a preference for pleasing his/her manager over meeting the demands of the customer. The second employee is customer focused; that is, favors meeting the customer's needs over pleasing his/her boss. Managing this role conflict can be quite complex and demanding.

In general terms, customer service and sales roles require different approaches to reduce the potential for role conflict. On the one hand, it is crucial for employees in the customer service interface to have the authority to make certain decisions for providing and maintaining good service. This is largely because customer service employees have an important role to play in creating and maintaining a positive impression of the business in the eye of the customer. In other words, they are ambassadors of the company. Consequently, having the freedom to make certain decisions in the interests of serving the customer will most likely create a good impression.

People working in sales, on the other hand, need to have adequate resources and a clear understanding of their role. They are primarily in the business of influencing the customer's decision to purchase their firm's product or service. In the sales role, meeting the demands of both the customers and the company is likely to be about negotiating on quality and price. It is important for the salesperson to understand his/her role and have the autonomy to negotiate. These two distinctive approaches are an important starting point for understanding and applying strategies to overcome role conflict in customer-focused work.

To have role clarity, employees need to be aware of their customer service priorities. This understanding of their priorities can come from several sources. For instance, role clarity can come from observing an experienced mentor, clear and regular lines of communication with their manager, or formal customer service training. Irrespective of how an employee learns the company's expectations, the greater their sense of role clarity, the more confident they will be in avoiding role conflict. Of course, all positions in companies will from time to time have conflicting expectations. Nevertheless, where clear priorities are established and effectively communicated, the employee has little difficulty in deciding on the appropriate course of action. Minimizing role conflict is the name of the game.

On the other hand, uncertainty on the part of a customer representative in carrying out their role can depend on a variety of factors. Two of the most common are a lack of managerial support and a confusing job description. Although it is difficult to completely eliminate ambiguity in customer roles, it can be significantly reduced by designing jobs to help customer representatives cope with it. For example, communicating the extent and limits of their authority in certain situations will assist employees in carrying out their role with more self-assurance. This involves consideration, empathy, and regular feedback on the manager's part. Managers will find it less frustrating and more rewarding to put their efforts behind strategies that reduce and/ or help employees cope with uncertainty in specific facets of their role. Staff too, will gain from role clarity.

In practice, what this means is that people working in customer-related roles need to meet frequently with their managers to sustain their role clarity. These meetings should be about discussing potential and real-life scenarios that may potentially place the employee in a difficult position. From these situations, policies and practices should be agreed upon to provide the employee with some guidelines within which to work when faced with a similar tight spot in future. These sessions are not supposed to be about managers communicating their organizational needs to their customer workers. To be effective, they should involve two-way communication and be based on developing ideas and strategies to overcome these potential dilemmas. The manager's responsibility in these sessions is to facilitate a problem-solving process with customer-facing workers in order to develop some practical guidelines for resolving real-life issues.

For example, if a customer calls to complain about being over-charged on their bill, the manager and employee can agree that if the discrepancy is under a certain amount, the employee can rectify the situation directly with the customer without consulting a manager, assuming of course that it is clear that the organization is at fault. This agreement between manager and employee can enable the employee to deal with the mistake quickly and confidently, and thereby minimize the damage. This is what I referred to as recovery speed in Chapter 3. If, after developing appropriate guidelines, these issues cannot be resolved in the field, the customer service representative can refer the matter to his/her manager. The most convenient and practical way to operationalize this process of reducing role conflict is to make these potential issues items for discussion at the weekly sales and customer service meetings, using real-life examples.

Rewards and incentives

There should be a clear link between an employee's role and the organization's reward structures. Conversely, a lack of role clarity for customer employees will most likely occur when there is nonalignment between company incentives and the particular requirements of the customer. For example, if management rewards customer service staff on the basis of how many customers they process (all things being equal), this is likely to lead to quicker processing of orders. However, if the role also requires spending time and attention on each particular customer's needs, this aspect of their role is likely to be neglected. A properly thought-out approach to rewards and incentives that is understood, consistent, and fair by all staff will maximize appropriate customer behavior and minimize role incongruity. As the cliché goes, this is easier said than done.

As a common illustration, how do you measure and reward the "people factor"? A customer worker's skill in the service sector may be reflected in knowledge, courtesy, competence, and communication abilities. These are all undeniable traits of quality service. These dimensions of customer service, albeit critical skills, are difficult to measure objectively. Even so, to reward desirable customer service behavior fairly and equitably, the following questions need to be asked and answered thoroughly:

- What behaviors define an appropriate customer-focused mindset?
- How is the company going to reward such behavior?
- When is the company going to reward such behavior?
- What should the reward be?
- How frequently should a reward be made?
- Who is going to decide whether it is appropriate behavior?

The answers to these questions will depend on the kind of industry and the nature of the company. A small cross-functional project team, representative of the overall business structure, could be set up to answer these questions. In this way, the rewards process is not being imposed on the company by management and is therefore more likely to gain buy-in.

AT THE COALFACE . . .

Cisco Systems is an American-based multinational corporation that designs and sells consumer electronics, networking and communications technology and services. Headquartered in San Jose, California, Cisco has more than 65,000 employees and an annual revenue of US $48.6 billion (as of 2013). Cisco is one of the world's biggest technology corporations and is considered an employer of choice.

Cisco fundamentally views technology as a means to an end. It is in the business of fixing customers' communication problems. And it uses technology to that purpose. Every employee, regardless of function or department, speaks directly with customers at least once a month. Even the human resources department, which in most companies is almost completely internal, had over two hundred visits from customers in 2001. Cisco's compensation model was altered to tie bonuses to customer satisfaction, as determined by an annual survey.

Cisco applied a five-point scale that measured customer satisfaction with all customer-facing operations across the company. Employee compensation is directly linked to the resulting overall scores. Annual bonuses were based on the level of customer satisfaction revealed in answers to one question: "What is your overall satisfaction with Cisco?" Each year a specific goal was set, and the size of the bonus was computed using the customer satisfaction multiplier along with a corporate revenue multiplier and salary multiplier. Employees have to think "outside the box."

Cisco administers the corporate customer satisfaction survey pre- and post-sales to customers who have bought both directly and indirectly through resellers from Cisco. The survey included business-focused questions, such as overall satisfaction with Cisco, and product-specific questions. Questions came from all corners of the company. Engineering, for example, used customer responses to its questions to drive specific product improvements.

Cisco receives the results online in real time and uses the information to locate obviously dissatisfied customers and to detect trends or potential challenges. This information empowered Cisco teams to follow up with their own customers to better understand any concerns or preferences and develop related action plans. Dissatisfied customers were almost always contacted to discuss not only their specific issues but also how Cisco could work with them to better resolve them.[1]

[1] Gulati, R. (2009) *Reorganizing for Resilience: Putting Customers at the Center of Your Business*. Boston, MA: Harvard Business Press.

Appropriate Information and Communication Technology (ICT) support structures are critical here too.

CRM

CRM as a business strategy helps a company integrate itself and forge a tight connection with the customer. In their haste to implement CRM systems, many companies have discovered that something with such a simple basis can be extremely difficult and expensive to implement successfully. Success requires more than simply buying new software and installing it in the sales centers. As a business strategy intended to gain market share and competitive advantage through improving customer loyalty, CRM has been discredited because of over-reliance on technology, and a reciprocal under-reliance on interpersonal communication. The successful implementation of a CRM strategy involves a holistic approach that scrutinizes the company's customer focus, its operations, systems, and culture. Customer relationship management therefore requires a mix of technical and human capabilities, and requires internal and external organizational attention.

Internally, CRM requires companies to quickly integrate all the information they have on a particular customer. Externally, businesses need to recognize and treat customers consistently and knowledgeably across channels, whether they reach you via a call center, website, catalog, or retail outlet. This critical enterprise-wide single view of the customer has been a major expense stumbling block for most businesses trying to manage their information in a multichannel environment.

Technically, CRM merges information with employees. Creating focused customer connections comes from several factors, including:

- databases that identify and track customers' preferences;

- dedicated account teams that build long-term relationships with targeted accounts; and
- involving customers in staffing, training, compensation, and communication practices.

To maximize customer knowledge, a company needs to have the capacity to link all customer information so that it is available to managers and customer service officers. Globalization is continually putting more and more pressure on the technical, human, and administrative resources of all organizations. Organizations that succeed over the next decade are likely to be leaner, with a crystal-clear focus on service delivery. At the same time, these successful companies will be required to do more with fewer resources and less time. On top of this, the ever-expanding explosion of information in the internet economy needs to be managed and analyzed. All this leads to challenges in creating and managing focused customer connections. A comprehensive and well implemented CRM system is critical for every business.

A CRM system is the important technological facet associated with creating a better connection with the customer. The CRM system needs to be implemented with four important considerations in mind. It must be:

- user-friendly;
- adaptable to the needs of the organization;
- cost-effective; and
- implemented as a strategy rather than a piece of software.

CRM software is one of the tools that help a company carry out this strategy. Depending on its implementation, it can help a business identify who its customers are, what they need, and anticipate what they may need in the future. It allows businesses to tailor offers to their current customers, and build closer relationships that make them feel valuable. It can help eliminate contact and data overlap between departments and improve consumer service. Overall, CRM can be an important way for a company to be more efficient and customer-friendly to capture greater market share, increase customer loyalty, and attract more customers.

What, then, are the critical steps in the successful implementation of a CRM system?

The implementation of a CRM system requires careful planning. The project should be split into four clearly defined phases:

Phase 1: Scoping and business needs assessment

Phase 2: CRM installation

Phase 3: Pilot

Phase 4: Training and skills transfer.

I will discuss each of these phases briefly.

Phase 1: Scoping and business needs assessment

This involves clarifying project roles and responsibilities with the service provider, the implementation of a proactive risk management strategy, milestone-driven processes, and resilience to change in project requirements. In order to assess business requirements, the service provider will need access to a selection of users and business managers to discuss their needs. The desired features, functionalities, and business drivers for project success need to be documented.

Phase 2: CRM installation

Once the scoping phase has been completed, costings for the project can be confirmed and the installation phase can begin. This phase will require the service provider to liaise with technical staff before installation to ensure there is a key understanding of the technical requirements and implications. Once installation is complete, configuration and development will be applied, with the service provider working on- or off-site, depending on the needs and desires of the business. During this phase, the service provider should work closely with managers and usability teams to ensure that the product is developed with rich, consistent functionality and minimal training requirements.

Phase 3: Pilot

Depending on timescales, a pilot should then be installed for a clearly defined number of users and initial training given to this group. The feedback from this phase should be used to update some systems before a complete rollout to all customer service staff.

Phase 4: Training and skills transfer

Thorough training is essential for the success of the project. Hands-on business-relevant training will be required, either through a "train the trainer" approach or through specifically designed training programs for end users. After the CRM project has completed its first life cycle, the service provider should host a follow-up workshop for all parties to review the project, voice opinions and questions, identify lessons learned, assess any skill gaps, and agree on the next steps. My experience is that, in their enthusiasm to reach full implementation, follow-up training is often neglected, or not done properly.

Careful and methodical planning of these four steps is important in CRM implementation.

Customer service training

Apart from CRM training, all employees should embark on a quality customer service training program. This program should not be an off-the-shelf training package. It should be tailored to the requirements of a particular business. This involves someone either inside the organization or an external consultant writing the program. Although many of the customer service concepts can be applied to any organizational setting, the examples, illustrations, application tools, and case studies need to be unique to the business. The program should also emphasize the importance and relevance of internal customer service as a basis for creating a customer-focused workplace culture.

For this to occur, it is advisable for all employees to participate in this training program. It may even be useful for some service providers that are external to the business to undertake the program too, so that they are more aware and appreciative of their role in servicing the requirements of the customer. Attendance at these training programs ought to be structured cross-functionally. In other words, participants in each training program should represent a slice of the organization; that is, one individual from the marketing department, one from production, one from finance, and so on. This will greatly contribute to cross-functional communication that elevates the relevance of internal customer service as a prelude to providing quality external service. Also, all new staff to the business, as part of their induction training with the company, should undertake this program. This training program needs to be more than a one-off. It is advisable that the program be conducted on an annual basis, and all staff be exposed to aspects of the program once a year as reinforcement.

For example, I conducted some customer service training with a well-known airline recently. We took vertical slices of the organization to constitute the training groups: We broke the company into groups of twelve, incorporating all the key functions of the airline. In each group we had representatives from sales and marketing, administration, pilots, flight attendants, and engineering and maintenance staff. I used a typical case of an airplane unexpectedly grounded due to mechanical difficulties. I facilitated a discussion in each workshop about what needed to be done by whom and when. For example, I asked the group, "Who makes the announcement to the passengers on board?" The pilots would typically suggest that it was the head flight attendant's responsibility. The flight attendants would counter this by saying that the pilot had more credibility and that in the first instance it should be the pilot who made the announcement. Maintenance and engineering indicated that they wanted a speedy and orderly disembarkation of passengers so that they could commence work on the mechanical problem. And so on. The result of these workshops was two-fold: clarity around everyone's role in this real-life situation and an appreciation of the perspectives of the various functions in the organization. The focus on these discussions was around minimizing inconvenience to the passengers.

What other elements impact on creating a customer-focused culture?

Three additional elements are important in developing a customer-focused culture. These are developing good internal customer service, the provision of adequate resources, and committed leadership.

An important and often neglected dimension of the value of customer focus is internal customers. Managers need to remember to clarify the roles of employees who do not have an external interface with customers. In particular, managers ought to clarify the role of support staff in their relationship with customer representatives. It is critical to break down the silo mentality that exists in most organizations. The silo mentality refers to an attitude found in some organizations that occurs when several departments or groups do not want to share information or knowledge with other individuals in the same company. A silo mentality reduces efficiency and can be a contributing factor to a failing corporate culture.

A lack of adequate resources can negatively affect the relationship between the customer and the company. By "resources," I mean things such as having available time to service customer requirements, having the right products and services available, and the support materials, product knowledge, and the authority to make certain decisions when dealing with the customer. All customer roles require these resources to be adequate and effective.

Finally, managers who have a genuine customer-focus mindset are in huge demand worldwide. They are required to deliver and implement these fundamental changes in thinking in businesses. Unfortunately, there is a shortage of people with these capabilities and experience at a senior level in the Western world. These managers are more often than not the catalysts for successfully driving the value of customer focus throughout a company. More than ever before, organizations need what are commonly referred to as transformational leaders. People with the right mindset and vision will continue to command a high premium, and will increasingly be valued over those who can only offer technical knowhow and expertise.

In spite of all these technical and human challenges, given support, incentives, skills, and growth opportunities by managers, modern employees are helping themselves (as well as their companies) by serving and fulfilling customers' needs. The traditional mindset of employees is one of pleasing their boss and playing organizational politics in the interests of their career; in other words, making the choice to satisfy the manager instead of the customer. This attitude exhibits the outdated value of internal focus, a characteristic of the conventional employment relationship. Being clear about who your customer is, and spending time providing value-added service, is a much more personally affirming use of an employee's time than wallowing in the internal ambiguity of a dying bureaucracy.

Organizations are better served by insisting that employees identify and measure their own value by servicing the needs and interests of their customers. To create this attitude, managers need to provide the necessary means by which employees can focus and assess their contribution to satisfying the customer's needs. Time and effort spent focusing internally by the manager or the staff member will ultimately detract from a customer-focus mindset.

Therefore, the appropriate individual reaction to the shared value of customer focus is to serve the customer before your manager (see the New Employment Relationship Model in Chapter 4). From an individual point of view, evidence of this mindset is a clear understanding and execution of their customer service role, particularly when they face (inevitable) conflict between the interests of the organization and the customer. It also entails three other traits: a respect for, and willingness to be motivated by, rewards and incentives for exceptional customer service behavior; confidence and skill in using the CRM system; and a willingness to attend and participate in customer skills development programs.

From the organization's perspective, the appropriate response to instilling the value of customer focus is to provide information, skills, and incentives to focus externally (see the New Employment Relationship Model in Chapter 4). Evidence of this includes a commitment from management to clarify potential conflicting situations for customer workers in their dealings with customers, the implementation of a fair and equitable rewards and incentives program, the implementation of a well thought-through CRM system, and relevant and timely customer service training opportunities. These individual and organization mindsets are likely to be characteristic of an organizational culture that has moved from a value of internal focus to a value of customer focus.

The **10** Key Points ...

 Customer focus is about focus: everything every employee and manager thinks, says, and does has the customer at the forefront of their mind. Customer service is the provision of quality service to a customer base within the confines of their company's policies and procedures.

The stumbling block for enhancing and maintaining customer focus is valid, reliable, and fair reward systems for exemplary customer-focused behavior; the development of new skills to deal with the customer interface; and restrictive career paths for customer workers.

There are four important elements to creating a customer-focused culture: (1) clear and understood customer workers' roles, responsibilities and priorities; (2) consistent, fair, and valid incentives for customer-focused behavior; (3) a comprehensive, well implemented, and utilized CRM system; and (4) tailored, timely, and relevant customer service training opportunities.

Any work with a customer places employees in the unique position of answering to two bosses: the organization and the customer.

There ought to be a clear link between an employee's role and the organization's reward structures.

Customer relationship management as a business strategy helps a company integrate itself and forge a tight connection with the customer.

The implementation of a CRM system requires careful planning. The project should be split into four clearly defined phases: (1) scoping and business needs assessment, (2) CRM installation, (3) pilot, and (4) training and skills transfer.

8 Customer service training should be completely tailored to the requirements of a particular business, and not an off-the-shelf package.

9 The appropriate individual reaction to the shared value of customer focus is to serve the customer before your manager.

10 The appropriate organizational response to instilling the value of customer focus is to provide information, skills, and incentives to focus externally.

The End of the Job

From job focus to performance focus

> *The modern employee, embracing a new mindset about their work performance, should acknowledge that who they are is not where they work, but what they do.*

John sat down with Peter to conduct his dreaded annual performance appraisal. John was anxious about this interview since he had some concerns about Peter's performance. In particular, John was concerned about Peter's lack of initiative, his poor team skills, and lack of commitment to developing his job skills. John didn't think Peter was performing well enough in this role. He had prepared thoroughly for the interview, with several examples to back up his concerns.

As Peter took his seat in John's office, John noticed that Peter had a copy of his job description clutched in his hand.

John got straight to the point. "Peter, I think you are doing your job well in lots of areas, but there are three areas I am concerned about."

"What are they?" asked Peter defensively.

"Well, first I am concerned that you don't show enough initiative in carrying out your work. For example, on Monday you complained to me that you

were short-staffed. However, I noticed that you were doing tasks that you could have delegated to other people. You need to show more initiative and do things differently," said John.

"But the need to be innovative is not stated anywhere in my job description," John fired back.

"And, the other day, you didn't help out in the production area when you finished your work load. That is not being a team player," Peter said.

"Once again, being a team player is not stated on my job description anywhere, John," Peter said in a challenging tone of voice.

"Also, I have been trying for months to get you to do that new course on report writing. You keep telling me that you've been too busy. Apart from anything else, John, it would help you develop your career skills," said Peter, trying to appeal to John's self-interest.

"I don't see developing my career skills written down anywhere on this job description," said Peter looking down at the two-page document in front of him.

John thought to himself that these job descriptions were a waste of time. Surely there was a better way to get Peter to focus on his performance in his role?

The old employment relationship emphasized a focus on the job. By "job," I mean the technical components of the work that needed to be done. It was more concerned with the *job* an employee did rather than the *role* they played within the organization.

Under the old system, managers and employees would evaluate their contribution to the organization on the basis of completing the literal requirements of the job description (JD). Employees— with some justification—would typically say, "If it's not on my JD, I'm not required to do it." Managers would carve out employees' responsibilities in a JD, as a way of maintaining control and means of monitoring staff performance. The JD was a fundamental building block of Frederick Taylor's scientific management approach.[1] The JD is another artifact of the traditional employment relationship—yet many organizations are still too reliant on this piece of paper.

What's wrong with a job description?

The truth is that employee performance in the modern work setting cannot completely be captured in a JD. Employees have two aspects to their work: job performance and non-job performance. Job performance encompasses those aspects of the job that can be documented in a JD. For example, it would include a breakdown of the various tasks the person is expected to perform in that particular job. Non-job performance is more to do with the role that person is expected to play within the work environment. For instance, most people would expect employees to show initiative when required to do so, be team players, and continually improve their skill set. These aspects are more related to the employee's organizational role. Yet they are not easily captured in the conventional JD despite being critical to performance.

From an organizational perspective, the non-job role employees play is now almost as important to a company's performance as job performance. It is now widely recognized that displaying team-work, contributing to improving the way the workplace functions, and developing one's work skills all have an important impact on organiza-tional performance. These three attributes are *displaying teamwork, contributing to improving the way the workplace functions, and developing one's work skills all have an important impact on organizational performance.*

---

[1] Taylor thought that, by analyzing work, the "one best way" to do it would be found. He would break down a job into its component parts and measure how long it took to do each, to the hundredth of a minute.

non-job specific and, as such, are rarely—if ever—mentioned in an employee's JD. In other words, employee work performance goes beyond the narrow confines of a JD and includes non-job specific behaviors.

Managers ought to recognize the significance and value of specific non-job behaviors with appropriate rewards and recognition. In terms of work, what is done is important, but so is how people go about it. Being innovative when needed, being a team player, and developing their skills are part of modern employees' organizational repertoire. Credit by the manager and willingness from the employee to contribute in ways beyond the scope of the JD shifts the focus beyond the job to performance.

How is performance focus different from job focus?

Everyone benefits from a performance-based organizational culture. One of the drivers now for employee success is the concept of value-adding to a job. Employees in the past were rewarded for their length of service. Those who stuck with the same company for a long time were entitled to certain privileges. Now companies want employees who are willing to add value in their role within their work setting, regardless of their tenure. This means that employees who contribute in constructive ways outside the range of their JD are more valuable than those who stick stringently to the letter of their JD. The issue of what constitutes job performance has been one of the most widely discussed concepts in HR management literature. It is only relatively recently that non-job behaviors have been universally considered to be critical to overall organizational performance.

Despite this focus on performance, most performance management systems are inadequate. These systems, more often than not, ignore dimensions of work performance that are not specifically job related. For instance, the conventional building block for performance systems, the JD, rarely mentions these non-job-related performance criteria. Value-added behaviors such as making suggestions for improvements, being a good organizational citizen, and displaying extraordinary customer service are often excluded from the JD. Yet they are all value-adding behaviors that inevitably contribute to organizational performance. I strongly advocate a broader interpretation of performance that goes beyond job-specific behaviors.

Job descriptions have traditionally focused only on the attributes of a specific job, which is normally broken down into six to eight job-related tasks. From my observations, this overreliance on JDs is still common in most public- and private-sector organizations. JDs continue to be defined by the explicit features of the job. They don't consider performance behaviors relevant to the organizational role. So, a more extensive model, factoring in both job- and non-job dimensions, is overdue. This continual emphasis on a job orientation in performance is the result of a need to create a legally defensible performance appraisal system.

Job descriptions driven by legal constraints do not stress the value and importance of performance that isn't task-related. But, in reality, work performance is two-dimensional, composed both of work required by a company and by discretionary employee work behaviors to complete those tasks. Task-based work required by the organization is usually covered in a well-crafted JD. But optional employee work activities such as the continuous improvement of systems and processes, exhibiting teamwork, and the capacity and willingness to grow and develop on the job, are undeniably valuable parts of performing in the workplace. This dimension of work is not formally documented in the conventional JD. Developing a two-dimensional model that recognizes the importance of non-task performance is critical in valuing overall organizational performance. This is referred to as *contextual performance*.

What is contextual performance?

Contextual performance covers multiple sub-dimensions of work such as teamwork, commitment, and the capacity to grow and develop. Although multidimensional models of performance that include job and non-job dimensions have been introduced in some companies, they lack a consistent and unifying framework across the general workforce. Without a common framework, there is little direction for managers to choose which dimensions of contextual performance to include (or exclude) from a performance appraisal system. This, understandably, leads to customized performance measures that emphasize specific job-related criteria only.

In reality, any job role consists of core or central features and peripheral or contextual features. Traditionally, measuring performance has neglected the value of these peripheral or contextual indicators, notwithstanding the acknowledgement that these intangible aspects of work do contribute to overall performance on the job. Performance systems that rely on evaluating only those work behaviors defined by a company as related to a specific job are narrow and, consequently, deficient.

The number of potential roles employees may take on at work is limitless. Some are consciously performed and others unconsciously carried out. Some are relevant, some not. Some take a split second to execute, some are ongoing. Some are appreciated, some not. Some are rewarded, some not. The question, therefore, is: What relevant and universally acceptable roles can employees play that are not directly associated with their particular job? The value placed upon these non-job roles varies from organization to organization and from leader to leader.

Which common work roles are valued universally?

Apart from the conventional job role, I suggest there are three non-job roles that are becoming increasingly important in any work situation. These are:

- team role;
- innovator role; and
- career role.

As discussed earlier, teams are becoming increasingly important in organizations, and being a team player is more important than ever before. Continuously improving processes and procedures is also increasingly a competitive advantage, and being innovative in carrying out tasks and responsibilities is critical to organizational performance. Finally, personal development and learning on the job is a key component for individual and organizational success.

Let's look at each of these three non-job roles briefly.

Team role

Teamwork will continue to be a critical component of organizational performance. Gainsharing plans and team-based incentives encourage team-based behaviors associated with being a team member, such as multi-skilling (see Chapter 5). The relevance of teamwork and its connection with performance is acknowledged widely in industry. Despite this recognition, the predominant basis for pay-for-performance still continues to be individual performance; although this is gradually changing.

Innovation role

Being enterprising and innovative is a trait of a successful employee, and is also increasingly valued by companies. Over thirty years ago, the prominent organizational theorist Edgar Schein predicted that, if firms intended to remain competitive in a complex and changing environment, they must have employees who are creative on behalf of an entire organization, not just creative in their job. More and more, employees are expected to behave in original ways, not just applying their creative skills to their specific jobs, but also contributing to the effectiveness and adaptability of their organization as a whole. Innovation is now an acknowledged factor in work performance. Many companies provide compensation incentives, such as gainsharing and cash rewards for constructive suggestions and entrepreneurial contributions. The only thing that has changed in the thirty years since Schein acknowledged employee innovation as a vital part of work performance is a greater relevance and appreciation of the innovator role in work performance.

Career role

Career enhancement by learning and growing in one's job is important to individuals and companies. This helps employees to maintain and increase the currency of their skill set and therefore their employability. Simultaneously, a more skilled and capable workforce is going to be an asset to any organization. Consequently, the career role is integral to overall performance. Indeed, some organizations today reward employees for career accomplishments either directly through pay increases, or indirectly by providing further career development opportunities. These rewards are often attached to training and educational accomplishments. For instance, skill-based pay is connected to the career role. These pay programs provide employees with bonuses or increases in their basic salary when they acquire new skills or attain further qualifications. A broad-based performance model that emphasizes learning and career development ought to replace a narrow work performance model that stresses job security and an organizationally-based career path.

Undoubtedly there are other contextual performance roles that are relevant to performance and could be considered in the realm of work performance. Nonetheless, these three additional dimensions of performance provide a useful starting point in viewing performance as a multidimensional concept that complements an employee's job role.

What are the benefits of a multidimensional model of performance?

It is hard to argue against the relevance of these three non-job roles to organizational performance. This multidimensional model addresses several weaknesses in the conventional appraisal of job performance. A multidimensional approach to performance has many advantages. Specifically:

- This model is multidimensional rather than one-dimensional, accounting for the multiple roles employees may take on in the workplace.
- Because this model accounts for multiple roles, it fills gaps associated with typical performance measures that only focus on the job role. For instance, someone can be technically proficient, but not be a team player. Or technically competent individuals may not add any value to their role, if they are disinclined to offer suggestions for continuous improvement in processes and systems and lack enterprise and initiative when needed. Such an individual may be unwilling to grow and develop on the job.
- The roles of team, innovation, and career (as described) are widely and progressively more recognized as vital dimensions of performance across most industries. Consequently, this multidimensional approach to performance has a broader, more

general, application than traditional measures of performance which are still—in most cases—too job specific.

- The three non-job roles can be applied to a broad range of industries and occupations.

Modern employees, embracing a new mindset about their work performance, should acknowledge that what they do is more important than where they work (see the New Employment Relationship Model in Chapter 4). What I mean by this is: an individual worker's sense of identity, self-esteem, and purpose should not necessarily be dependent on their connection to the organization. When an individual allows their identity to wholly reside with their workplace, they become organizationally dependent. On the surface, that may not seem to be a problem. But this mindset locks employees into a permanent victim relationship, perpetually subservient to the company. This creates problems around performance. For instance, employees with this attitude are unlikely to speak up in meetings for fear of creating an unfavorable impression.

Instead of this outlook, contemporary employees are better served by viewing their skills and self-esteem as portable and not dependent on any particular organizational setting. It is also in the interests of organizations now to foster independent relationships with their workforce so that they reap the benefits of free thinking and uninhibited contributors in organizational outcomes. Employees who are willing to constructively question established approaches and practices and offer alternative ways of doing things, are likely to be more valuable organizational members. Benefits, status symbols, and policies that favor tenure over performance and internal pleasing over customer service are characteristics of the old value of job focus. If the company's efforts are in any way distracted from doing quality work in the service of customers, it diminishes overall performance. I pointed out in Chapter 6 that independent, performance-focused employees who look outward towards their customers will increasingly be in greater demand by companies. These independently-minded employees are the key to a robust commercial future.

Performance-based work starts with changing the focus from remunerating employees on the basis of time spent on the job to remuneration based on the achievement of KPIs. These KPIs should cover both job and non-job roles. The old saying, a fair day's work for a fair day's pay, is no longer applicable in the new reality.

What can be specifically done to change from a job focus to a performance focus?

The first important step in moving towards a performance-focused culture is to change JDs to role descriptions (RDs) for all employees in the organization. What's the difference between a JD and RD?

Job descriptions usually define a set of specific tasks and responsibilities that are performed by a particular job-holder. Specific tasks are usually expressed in terms of outputs; for example, "to maintain filing and record systems." They tend to specify a narrow set of behaviors defined as a job. They typically include the employee characteristics required for competent performance of the job. However, a JD usually describes and focuses on the job itself, not on any specific individual who might undertake that particular job.

An RD, on the other hand, is concerned with elements such as which groups or areas the position serves, the end accountabilities of the role, and the overall skills and abilities required for the specific type of work. When viewed from this perspective, a number of jobs can often be grouped into a role because, while tasks and specific goals may differ, the overall purpose, elements, and skills or competencies required are very similar.

Role descriptions define the organizational role of the individual and link these with KPIs. A role is a more generalized description of what is required in a job for effective performance; that is, what the individual needs to bring in terms of skills, knowledge, and behavior. The focus is therefore on inputs. Role descriptions are less likely to define the activities of the job and more likely to define the performance criteria of the role in the context of a particular workplace. As I mentioned, the same RD can be applicable to a number of different jobs where, even though the tasks are different, the inputs required are essentially the same.

For example, consider a production engineer with a designated work site and structure. Apart from the specifics of the work site and structure, this job plays a similar role to other production engineers stationed at other sites. Therefore, it may make sense to develop one production engineer role document rather than have a JD for each site. Doing this streamlines the documentation, meaning that fewer documents are required. The role document consequently focuses on role similarities, rather than job differences, and provides more flexibility for both the individual and the organization. Employees then have the scope to take on new assignments and tasks within the same role, or move into similar roles in different areas of the company. Organizations, on the other hand, have the capacity of being more flexible and responsive to changing market trends.

I have quite a lot to say about changing JDs to RDs in one of my previous books: *The End of the Performance Review: A New Approach to Appraising Employee Performance.*[2]

An RD, on the other hand, adds a layer of accountability. Apart from including the specific tasks and responsibilities related

---

[2] Baker, T.B. (2013) *The End of the Performance Review: A New Approach to Appraising Employee Performance.* London: Palgrave Macmillan. This book may be purchased from www.winnersatwork.com.au.

to the technical requirements of the job, the RD considers the non-job roles the employee is expected to play. Role descriptions define the organizational role of the individual, not just their job responsibilities.

Earlier in this chapter, we looked at three non-job roles that are undoubtedly applicable to all jobs across all industries. These were team role, innovator and continuous improvement role, and career role. Specifically, let's consider the following elements of the employee's non-job role that cover team, career, and innovation responsibilities and which are to be taken into account in an RD.

Team role

In the context of the team role, leadership, accountability, collaboration, and communication are key elements.

Leadership

Leadership characteristics should consider the ability to influence others within the organization in a positive way. For instance, this element of the non-job role may cover the impact the employee has on improving processes, outcomes, and efficiencies. It also includes the degree of involvement the employee has in team meetings, and his/her capacity to be solution-focused.

Accountability

Accountability includes the degree to which employees accept responsibility for their own work and the work of others. This non-job attitude ought to take into consideration the impact of a position's end results on the work unit, function, or organization as a whole and those it serves. It covers the degree of autonomy in decision making required for an employee to be successful in his/her role.

Collaboration

Collaboration is concerned with the ability to produce successful outcomes by working cooperatively with others. For instance, an important aspect of collaboration is sharing relevant information and soliciting input and assistance from others. Other non-job components include the capacity to integrate input and seek consensus to reach organizational goals. To collaborate effectively, an employee may need to understand team processes and be able to apply problem-solving techniques.

Communication

Communication in a non-job context refers to the ability to effectively interact and exchange information with other members of the organization and external stakeholders, such as suppliers. More specifically, effective communication includes developing factual and logical presentation of ideas and opinions using both written and oral skills, and demonstrating effective listening skills.

Innovation and continuous improvement role

Problem solving, critical thinking, and customer responsiveness are important elements of the innovation and continuous improvement role.

Problem solving and critical thinking

These traits of contextual performance are associated with continuously seeking to identify, define, critically analyze, and resolve work problems through researching and testing alternative ideas and approaches. Thus, these non-job roles involve thinking outside traditional parameters, and using innovative and creative ideas and actions to improve work processes and services to internal and external stakeholders. The appropriate mindset to accomplish this is one of seldom settling for a service or process that is "good enough." In being innovative and creative, employees take measured risks in their work to add value and enhance the achievement of the company's mission.

Customer responsiveness

Customer responsiveness involves the ability to identify, understand, build relationships with, and adapt to the requirements of external and internal customers in an appropriate manner—that is, in keeping with the goals and values of the company while demonstrating fiscal responsibility. This element requires employees to do more than simply follow standard processes and procedures. Employees need to know, and respond to, the expectations of customers, focusing particularly on quality and timeliness of service. To do this, employees need to continually improve their approaches and be prepared to introduce completely new procedures when required.

Career role

A willingness to develop personally and technically are key elements for personal and organizational success in the context of the career role.

Self-development

Developing oneself is associated with the commitment to help in carrying out employment duties now and in the future. To do this, employees ought to demonstrate evidence of actively seeking out appropriate opportunities to expand work-related knowledge, skills, and experiences.

Technical development

Technical development is the second aspect of career development. It involves individuals planning and making decisions about education, training, and career choices as well as developing the right skills and knowledge to do so. Looking for and taking up opportunities to enhance technical skills within and outside the organization is ultimately the responsibility of the individual.

The above list of elements associated with the three non-job roles is by no means exhaustive. However, it provides HR professionals with a good starting point for considering contextual performance in the workplace. The conventional JD does not normally incorporate these elements. An RD, on the other hand, recognizes these characteristics as integral to work performance and explicitly makes reference to them.

These non-job responsibilities are supplementary to the core functional competencies associated with a person's job. They address the multidimensional aspects of organizational performance. A complete and accurate RD is very important for classification, performance planning, and performance management. Collecting data on these non-job roles is an important preliminary step when moving from a job focus to a role focus.

Which approaches are available to formulate role descriptions?

The process for completing an RD is directly connected to its quality and accuracy. The key to successfully writing an RD is collaboration between manager and employee, among fellow employees, and across hierarchical levels.

Several collaborative approaches are outlined below to compile the information necessary for the development of an accurate RD.

Dynamic duo method

With this approach, the manager or supervisor chooses two individuals who perform the same role—for example, two accounts receivable clerks—to consider the non-job elements associated with their role. Following this discussion, a document is written, reflecting more than one perspective of the role. The manager or supervisor discusses and modifies the role document in partnership with the two employees, providing a third perspective.

Team method

In this approach, the manager or supervisor chooses three or four individuals, all of whom perform the same role, to complete the document. This method is particularly useful when a role has many incumbents, or when the role can be found in several departments, calling for multiple viewpoints. Teams should be kept small, as groups larger than three or four employees can have difficulty reaching consensus and are much slower to complete the task of defining the elements of the non-job roles. The manager or supervisor then reviews and discusses the document with the whole team.

Supervisor–incumbent method

In this case, the supervisor or manager works with a single employee to complete the role documentation. This method is particularly effective when an employee is new to a role within the company, in cases where there are concerns about performance or understanding of the role's components, or where the role is undergoing major content changes. This method involves a similar review and approval process to the team method.

Single-employee method

In the single-employee method, the employee completes the document him/herself. For roles with only one employee, or for a vacant/new position, this may be the only method available, but it is not collaborative, and therefore is the least preferred method. A review by the manager and the senior staff person for the area (if applicable) is critical when using this method, in order to provide a broader perspective.

The process just described, using any of the methods outlined above, is referred to as a *role analysis*. An accurate role analysis is an important first step in creating a performance-focused workplace culture.

What is role analysis?

Role analysis is the process of collecting, analyzing, and recording information about the requirements of a role in order to create a role profile. Role analyses focus on the demands made on role holders in terms of what they need to know and be able to do to deliver the expected level of performance.

From an individual perspective, the key purpose in conducting a role analysis is to describe a job as it is actually performed, and understand the job well enough to reliably and accurately define worker requirements. Done well, a role analysis is the best way to provide the most relevant position-specific information, which may then be used in a variety of HR functions, including recruitment and selection, performance management, and assessment.

From an organizational perspective, a role analysis helps to create a shared view of a job, fostering greater acceptance among all parties of the job's actual interpretation. It also provides documentation that allows the employer to record and defend processes and decisions, should they be challenged.

Some guidelines for completing role analyses include:

- training should be given to all those involved in analyzing and evaluating jobs and roles;
- agreeing on a format for how RDs, specific to the needs of the organization, are to be written, to enable work roles to be assessed to a common standard;
- drawing up a representative sample of people from the spread of jobs to be covered by the role;
- selecting the facilitators of job evaluation panels for their knowledge of job evaluation, their impartiality, and their concern that decisions of the panel are not discriminatory;
- not overly relying on generic JDs, especially when there are significant clear variations in job duties; and
- removing gender, race, and individual identification from role profiles.

Once these JDs have been converted to RDs, KPIs and targets can be established for each key performance area (KPA). These documents will become the cornerstone of a performance management framework.

What is a performance management framework?

A *performance management framework*, shown in Figure 7.1, illustrates the relationship between RDs and the performance management structure of a company.

The performance management framework shows the links between the key elements essential to the management of performance in an

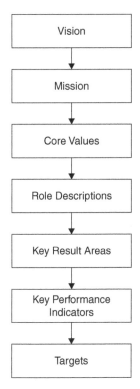

FIG 7.1 / Performance management framework[3]

organization. The *vision* is a broad statement related to the direction in which the organization is heading. It answers the question: What does the business aspire to in future? For example, Bill Gates' vision for Microsoft is "to have a personal computer on every desk running Microsoft." The *mission* is a broad statement relating to how we intend to achieve our vision. It answers the question: How are we going to achieve our vision? For example, Dell Computers' mission is: "We are able to provide customers with superb value;

[3] Baker, T.B. (2009) *The 8 Values of Highly Productive Companies: Creating Wealth From a New Employment Relationship*. Brisbane: Australian Academic Press.

high-quality technology; customized systems; superior service and support; and product services that are easy to buy and use." The *core values* describe the key behaviors needed to achieve the mission. One example could be, "Respect, which means that we respect the needs of our customers." The *RDs*, as we have discussed, explain the organizational role employees are expected to play in meeting the vision, mission, and core values of the organization. The *key result areas* (KRAs) identify the job and non-job dimensions of performance. *Key performance indicators* are the qualitative and quantitative ways that KRAs will be measured in terms of performance. *Targets* are the precise minimum standard of performance for each KPI. Each aspect of the performance management framework is linked. In this way, what people do in the workplace has context.

Once KRAs, KPIs, and targets have been identified and include job and non-job behaviors, valid and reliable reward structures can be put in place to reinforce a focus on performance. This rewards and incentives system can be either monetary or non-monetary, or a combination of the two.

AT THE COALFACE . . .

New Zealand dairy company Fonterra has a people management process called PERFORMplus for salaried employees. The process incorporates success-related and desirable job- and non-job Fonterra competencies, values, and objectives for remuneration and opportunities for career development. Key performance indicators are identified and agreed between staff and management each year in annual incentive plans. These relate to operational, financial, and qualitative measures from a three-year strategic plan and annual budget.

The Australian National Maritime Museum's 2012–2015 strategic plan was built around five KRAs. Within each of these were several KPIs. For instance, the KPI that 90 percent of stories in the media about the museum should be positive is part of the KRA of extending the museum's profile and partnerships. Most of the KPIs are specifically quantified—but not all are. A KPI for profile and partnerships is that the museum is acknowledged as a preeminent and innovative cultural institution. This requires employees to exhibit their innovativeness in what they say, think, and do every day on the job.

From the organization's perspective, and referring back to the New Employment Relationship Model discussed in Chapter 4, the proper response to instilling the value of performance focus is to link rewards and benefits with performance, rather than organizational dependency. Evidence of this includes incentives on the part of the company to acknowledge the relevance and importance of team-based behavior, skill enhancement, and innovation and entrepreneurial contributions. In a shared sense, the individual's responsibility is to focus on what they do, not where they work. Evidence of this includes a willingness and commitment to play their role in the non-job dimensions of team-based behavior, skill enhancement, and innovation and entrepreneurial contributions. These individual and organization mindsets are likely to be characteristic of an organizational culture that has moved from a value of job focus to a value of performance focus.

The **10** Key Points …

1. Employee performance in the modern work setting cannot completely be captured in a job description.

2. It is now widely recognized that the non-job roles of displaying teamwork, contributing to improving the way

the workplace functions, and developing one's work skills have an important impact on organizational performance.

3 Most performance management systems are inadequate; they more often than not ignore dimensions of work performance that are not specifically job related.

4 Job descriptions have traditionally focused only on the attributes of a specific job, which is normally broken down into six to eight job-related tasks.

5 Role descriptions define the organizational role of the individual and link these with KPIs.

6 Role descriptions cover such elements as leadership, accountability, collaboration, communication, self-development, innovation, problem solving and critical thinking, and customer service.

7 There are four methods for collecting data for a role description: dynamic duo, team, supervisor–incumbent, and single-employee.

8 Role analysis is defined as the process of collecting, analyzing, and recording information about the requirements of roles in order to provide the basis for a role profile.

9 From the organization's perspective, the appropriate response to instilling the value of performance focus is to link rewards and benefits with performance, rather than organizational dependency.

10 From an employee's perspective, the appropriate response to the value of performance focus is to focus on what they do, not where they work.

8

Burn the Organizational Chart!

From functional-based to project-based work

> *People are by nature tribal; that is, they naturally build alliances and associations with others.*

The newly appointed CEO, Melissa, identified her first major challenge on the job as the need to break down the boundaries between departments in the government agency. She had observed that the agency was organized around several "silos." It was a functionally-based organization. This was evident at the senior management level. The most important cross-functional team, the senior management team, was disjointed and did not operate as a team. Managers would come to executive meetings with their functional hat on and fail to consider issues from the perspective of the overall organization. Melissa knew she had her work cut out in breaking down these traditional departmental boundaries.

She observed that the level of cooperation between these departments was minimal, even nonexistent is some cases. She was determined to change this. She reviewed the organizational structure, which was based on hierarchy and segmented across several functions.

Melissa decided to implement a number of cross-functional project teams. She reflected this in the organizational chart. For instance, one team was formed to look at improving communication across the organization. Representatives were selected from all departments. Another cross-functional project team was set up to review systems and processes.

Peter was invited from the marketing department to serve on one of these project teams by the CEO. He seemed quite excited about being chosen, recognizing the need to improve cross-functional communication within the organization. Peter had been approached directly by the CEO. He went to talk to the marketing manager in her office. Mary was less than enthusiastic when Peter told her about this development.

"I wish the CEO had spoken to me first," Mary said to Peter. "I can't afford to release you to attend these 'talk fests.' Peter, you are too valuable to the department. We are already short-staffed. How often does she want you to attend these meetings?"

"I don't know," replied Peter. "She hasn't told me."

"Well, it sounds like a complete waste of time. Your primary responsibility is to my department, Peter," said Mary. "You're a critical person in this department, and I'll have to speak to the CEO about this and let her know my feelings."

Peter left Mary's office deflated and confused. He had thought that this was a great opportunity to break down the silos in the organization and improve communication across the organization. He couldn't understand his boss's reaction.

The traditional hierarchically structured organization has served us well for two hundred years. But the functionally-based organizational structure is generally pretty inflexible and slow to change direction. It is unsuitable for the twenty-first century. Organizations structured around divisions, departments, units, branches, or sections are less responsive to fluctuations in market conditions. They were suitable for the twentieth century, with its reasonably stable marketplace, but organizations structured around functions are less appropriate in today's fast-paced and unpredictable marketplace. Cross-functional communication is slower and therefore response time is also slower in this kind of environment. The nature of work today, as we have discussed, is more project-based than functional. Most issues need quick input from several sources within an organizational structure. A new kind of organizational structure is needed.

Employees and employers now have to shift their mindset from functional-based to project-based work.

What is project-based work?

A project-based team is a group of employees from various functional areas of the organization who are all focused on a specific cross-functional project. For example, members of a specific project team may come from various departments, such as engineering, marketing, finance, human resources, and operations. As a team, they are responsible for working together to improve coordination and innovation across traditional divisions or departments and to resolve mutual problems between company functions.

Project-based work can be organized in two ways. Temporary or ongoing project teams can be set up to do this work. Ad hoc or temporary project teams exist for a set period of time, and ongoing project teams are long-term with a relatively stable membership. The use of project teams, whether temporary or longstanding, provides organizations with adaptable and flexible structures. They can supplement—rather than replace—functional work groups. Project teams are characteristic of a network organizational structure.

AT THE COALFACE . . .

Deloitte is one of Australia's largest professional services firms, with 3,200 employees providing audit, tax, consulting, and financial advisory services. The CEO, Giam Swiegers, personally created some temporary cross-functional teams in late 2005. These temporary teams were a key driver of the firm's cultural diversity initiatives. The project teams were designed to learn from the ideas and challenges of the culturally diverse workforce. The data gained from the teams led to the establishment of an initiative aimed at attracting and retaining talented employees. Head of People and Performance at Deloitte, Alec Bashinsky, implemented "Tiger Teams"—cross-functional teams of people and performance managers—to align HR and business strategy. Each team managed a specific HR strategy or program in the organization. Across the organization, there was an emphasis on "inspirational behavior" by leaders (measured by surveys) and mutual responsibility for the firm's "people strategy." The organization has seven "signals" that guide behavior. They are: "we recruit and retain the best, talk straight, play to win and think globally, grow and improve, aim to be famous, empower and trust, and have fun and celebrate."[1]

---

[1] Deloitte, "Culture and beliefs." At www.hcamag.com/profiles/deloitte-putting-the-people-in-performance-113536.aspx, accessed January 2014.

What is a network organizational structure?

An organization that is structured around project teams, whether temporary or ongoing, can be referred to as a networking organization. A networking organization is more flexible and maneuverable than a bureaucracy. Unlike a bureaucracy, which has a fixed set of relationships for processing all problems, the network organization moulds itself to each problem. This kind of organizational arrangement adapts over time by the interactions of problems, people, and resources within the broad confines of corporate strategy rather than by top management directives. The networking organization is a post-bureaucratic organizational structure.

A networking organization is a social network that is integrated across formal functional boundary structures. Interpersonal ties are formed without regard for functional departments. The structure of a network organization changes from a hierarchical to a flat form. Work is organized around projects rather than functions. This approach makes sense: most of the work we do in organizations is not done in isolated silos. For instance, elements of processing a customer request are likely to be dealt with in several departments. The sales department wins an account and the customer service department may process the order. Once the order has been finalized, customer service passes this information to production. The production department then informs the finance department, which invoices the customer once the product has been packaged and sent by the dispatch function of the business. Most of the work we do transcends departmental boundaries.

As I have mentioned many times, employees are more likely now to complete tasks in teams. Work has changed from being fragmented to team-oriented. This requires a completely different mindset. Traditionally, the appropriate mindset was to think of work in functional terms: "I have a specific job to do and my job is to do that well." More apt thinking now is along the lines of playing an important role as part of a team to achieve a certain task. This project team will most likely consist of people from a variety of functions. Of course, the function-based attitude is still prevalent in many organizations, with employees doing their work "with their blinkers on."

The evolution of the network organization is a response to the drivers of change discussed in Chapters 1 and 2. These drivers include heightened competition arising from a globalized marketplace, the transition from a production-based to service-based economy, and the shift to a service orientation. In practice, this means that companies are doing more with less: their revenues are increasing as the size of organizations is decreasing. Leading companies are developing structures that are improving quality and adding greater value while reducing cycle time. One of the key elements of these corporate transformations has been the manner in which people are utilized.

Above all, one of the tasks of leaders of the new organizational structure is to make effective use of the "intellectual capital" of individuals to achieve some advantage over their competitors. A combination of valuing individual enterprise on the one hand and improved cross-functional communication on the other is the challenge for leaders today. This balancing act means valuing both individualism within and connectivity across the organization. This is the essence of shifting from a shared value of functional-based to project-based work.

How do we shift from a function to project identity?

Employees' organizational identity has traditionally been tied up with their functional area. People have built relationships with colleagues in their department and are accountable to a functional boss. One of the key challenges in moving to a network organizing structure is to replace this functional identity with a cross-functional team identity. This cross-functional team identity is defined as the extent to which employees identify with the team rather than with their functional areas.

AT THE COALFACE . . .

Organizations need to make many decisions about their structure, for example whether functions such as human resource management would be better handled by a central group of functional experts, or spread out among various divisions. Some organizations, like Coca-Cola, have a central functional HR hub but many of the HR activities are assigned to line managers in the divisions. The divisional manager knows the workplace and the people and can respond to the specific needs of their divisions. At the same time, they benefit from the policy and systems established by HR.

In a network organization, individuals perceive that they have a greater stake in the success of the cross-functional team than their functional department. This kind of allegiance is different from social cohesion. Whereas social cohesion or unity is associated with teamwork and harmony, team identity refers to the extent to which an individual feels their work identity belongs with a particular team or group. Under the traditional bureaucratic organizational structure, employees identify with their functional area or department. In the network organization, the individual has a greater commitment to cross-functional groups and teams. Restructuring the organization from a bureaucratic operation to a network approach is not the whole answer. Fostering new team identities also has to be addressed.

People are by nature tribal; that is, they naturally build alliances and associations with others. So, within organizations, it is natural for people to form groupings with other employees. The formal groupings in organizations are traditionally organized around departments. When groups are formed formally or informally, they differentiate themselves from others by creating physical and/or psychological boundaries. This is to protect their team identity. Physical boundaries can be doorways, buildings, or passageways. Psychological boundaries are not necessarily visible or tangible but are, nevertheless, real. They include such characteristics as developing specific plans and direction, implementing systems and approaches unique to the team, building networks with other stakeholders outside the team, and celebrating team successes. These physical and psychological boundaries can be helpful or unhelpful for an organization.

Useful psychological boundaries can be formed around teams through particular activities and strategies. We will discuss these shortly. Sometimes these boundaries develop unconsciously. For instance, a team which is homogeneous in some way, such as similar age, familiar background and experience, or from a racial minority, may feel a sense of identity and belonging and protect itself from the "outside world" by looking out for one another. Nothing is said: it just happens. But team leaders can fashion these boundaries deliberatively. Apart from developing team identity, psychological boundaries can be formed to protect the team from negative or destructive outside influences and to manage the team's interactions with various stakeholders outside the team.

What psychological boundaries are there?

Research has validated at least three types of boundary activities.[2] There are no doubt others, but these three are a useful starting point. They are referred to as:

- buffering;
- spanning; and
- bringing up boundaries.

From research findings, these three boundary-spanning activities transfer downward from the formal organizational structure to the

[2]Yang, A. & Louis, M.R. (1999) "Migration of organizational functions to the work unit level: Buffering, spanning, and bringing up boundaries." *Human Relations* 52(1), 25–47.

work unit level when organizations are transforming from hierarchical to network organizing structures. In practice, how do these boundary activities manifest themselves to protect the new identity of the team? Each of the three boundary activities is briefly defined below.

Buffering

Buffering is a strategy used by team members to build and protect the team's unique identity. This strategy emphasizes the need to protect the team from outside forces that are perceived by the team members to be threatening. These outside forces may or may not be a threat to the team. But if the team members perceive them to be so, they are likely to take buffering action. By taking certain actions, the team is able to function more efficiently and effectively. Practical activities to buffer include:

- forecasting, planning, and preparing for the future;
- deflecting work that may disrupt the team's core activities to other teams or organizational units;
- stockpiling human, technical, and administrative resources; and
- developing systems for processing the team's work.

Managers who encourage and support these activities will assist their team, whether it is functional or cross-functional, to shape a distinctive identity. Some practical initiatives include:

- encouraging and supporting team planning and forecasting;
- coordinating workflow throughout the team;
- encouraging the team to be as self-sufficient as possible in their resourcing; and
- supporting the team to develop their own unique systems and processes.

By promoting, supporting, and encouraging these kinds of activities, managers do not allow outside pressures, demands, and interference to adversely affect their team's output.

Boundary spanning

While buffering is an internal defense mechanism to protect the team, boundary spanning is activities that reach out to critical people and resources outside the team. Boundary-spanning activities are designed to maintain existing and build new interdependent relationships within and outside the organization to guarantee the team's relevance, or reason for existence.

Team member activities that can be classified as boundary spanning include, but are not limited to, the following:

- promoting and encouraging communication, bargaining, and negotiation between the team and other critical teams and individuals;
- seeking external support and contracting important outside assistance; and
- building and maintaining alliances within and outside the organization with influential stakeholders.

By promoting, supporting, and encouraging these kinds of activities, managers are sustaining their team's significance, or justifying its reason for existing.

Positive corresponding management initiatives to encourage and support boundary spanning include, but are not limited to, the following:

- encouraging and supporting team members to build relationships with teams that will help them achieve their objectives;
- assisting the team to network and seek out assistance and support beyond the team when needed; and
- supporting team members to build constructive alliances with influential stakeholders within and outside the business.

By promoting, supporting, and encouraging these kinds of activities, managers help their team to strengthen their reason for being.

Bringing up boundaries

Bringing up boundaries involves two primary functions: (1) creating and maintaining a common vision for tasks performed by the team, and (2) building and sustaining a shared team culture. In contrast to buffering, where the energy largely goes into keeping out external forces that might interrupt and distract the work unit, bringing up boundaries is focused on attracting the energies of team members to the unit's task by utilizing and containing resources available within the work unit. Unlike spanning activities, where the effort is made to import the critical resources from the external environment, bringing up boundaries entails shaping and applying internal resources to the goals of the team. For example, team-based activities include but are not limited to the following:

- promoting and coordinating multi-skilling team members so that they can perform several tasks within the confines of the team (see Chapter 5);
- forming a distinctive team values charter; and
- encouraging the team to celebrate their successes.

By promoting, coordinating, and encouraging these kinds of activities, managers are assisting their team to construct and maintain a common vision and a shared team culture.

Some specific practical initiatives include:

- facilitating the flexible deployment of team members' skills in the form of a multi-skilling program;
- facilitating a team-building session that focuses on articulating their own identity and values; and
- organizing and promoting team celebrations when milestones have been met.

By facilitating, organizing, and promoting these kinds of activities, managers are assisting their team to clarify their vision and create a unique team-based culture.

I think it is misguided for organizational leaders to assume that transforming from a traditional bureaucratic to network organization abolishes psychological boundaries altogether. It does not. What happens is the traditional boundaries (which we commonly refer to as silos) reform themselves in other ways. If the organization changes to a flatter structure that puts a priority on cross-functional communication, then the boundaries will probably eventually be shaped around cross-functional project teams. It is important to remember that people are by their nature tribal and as such will want to belong to a tribe. That is unavoidable when a group of people come together for a sustained period of time. The real question for managers is: Are the boundaries in our company helpful or unhelpful in pursuing desirable organizational output?

Managers should break down the psychological and physical boundaries that make the company rigid and unresponsive to market forces. But they are wrong if they think that they can restructure an organization with no tribes. So, if the response to the question above is that the current boundaries are unhelpful, then the second question needs to be: How can we reconfigure boundaries to make the company more flexible and responsive?

During any large-scale change management process or organizational transformation, many new boundary-related activities emerge. Some of these activities are obstructive. Therefore managers need to deliberately manage boundaries. With an awareness of these three boundary protection strategies at the team level, managers have a useful framework for shaping healthy new cross-functional boundaries that supplement the move to a network organizational structure. Employees also benefit, as this gives them a new team identity on which to build their talents and abilities.

What are the elements of the shared value of project-based work?

Similar to the other seven values in the model, instilling the shared value of project-based work in the culture of an organization is a collaborative effort between employer and employee. Through its leadership, the organization should promote, support, and encourage boundary-spanning behavior in cross-functional teams rather than at the functional level. This includes the implementation of practical initiatives that are consistent with the three types of boundary activities: buffering, boundary spanning, and bringing up boundaries. For these activities to be successful in promoting project-based work, employees in these teams have a role to play too. Essentially, employees who are ready to work cross-functionally will most likely identify with their cross-functional team before their functional department. Moreover, employees will respond positively to these management initiated boundary activities. The shared value of project-based work is the support for and readiness to engage in boundary activities at the cross-functional team level.

As a first step, the organization needs to be restructured to accommodate a cross-function organizational structure with far less emphasis on the traditional functional structure.

How do you create a cross-functional organizational structure?

Most organizational charts still illustrate their organizational structure as hierarchical and functional. Figure 8.1 is an example of a typical functional formation.

This traditional organizing approach creates two challenges. First, this functional arrangement, which is based on a departmental or

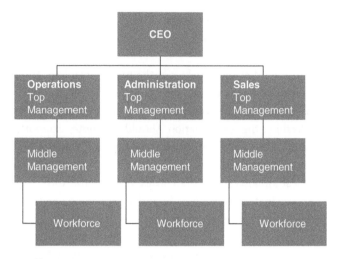

FIG 8.1 / A traditional organizational structure

divisional structure, encourages a silo mentality. These divisions are usually organized around functions such as operations, administration, and sales, as reflected in Figure 8.1. Each function traditionally has its own identity led by a functional leader, and thus cross-functional communication is stifled. Through traditional boundary management activities, these functions insulate themselves from other functions within the company.

The second dilemma faced by this hierarchical arrangement is that accountability for performance is contained within each function or discipline. In other words, the workforce in a particular department or division is answerable to a line manager or middle manager within that function and they, in turn, are answerable to their top manager. As a consequence, there are very few, if any, cross-functional accountabilities in these established structures. While this functional paradigm has been a successful organizing process for at least a century, I think it has done more to impede customer-focused business performance improvement over the past two decades than any other single factor. For these reasons, a new organizing structure is overdue.

In contrast to Figure 8.1, Figure 8.2 illustrates a more flexible and responsive organizational structure, based on the cross-functional paradigm.

As Figure 8.2 shows, this new structure still has functions. However, there is an additional organizing structure (project-based teams). These teams are cross-functional entities whose members comprise representatives from several departments. Project-based teams strengthen cross-functional communication and disperse accountability beyond the functions. Also, instead of the traditional top-down hierarchy, the cross-functional paradigm is structured around the management team which promotes two dimensions of accountability: cross-functional as well as functional. Figure 8.2 illustrates this two-dimensional approach to organizational accountability. Note that Figure 8.2 has no spokes (functional boundaries) within the managerial space. This structure invites managers to think like

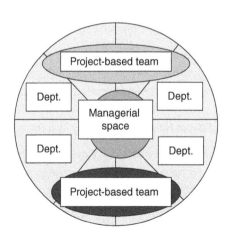

FIG 8.2 / A cross-functional organizational structure

organizational leaders rather than as heads of divisions, departments, or business units.

How do you create cross-functional teamwork?

Aside from creating a new organizational structure, to maximize the potential of cross-functional teams through boundary activities, six important issues need to be addressed by managers and team members. These are:

1. Proper project team membership.
2. A clear charter and purpose.
3. The right connections.
4. Achievable, noticeable results.
5. Understood and agreed-upon ground rules.
6. Intensive team-building upfront.

I explain each of these boundary activities briefly below.

Proper project team membership

Membership of any team is crucial to its success. When selecting team members, managers need to consider three important questions:

1. Do potential members have expertise in the project the team will be dealing with?
2. Does the team have "political pull" that can help it fulfill its charter?
3. Can the employees function effectively as a team?

The first question can be challenging. Expertise can be a sticky issue. If all team members have substantial expertise in the problem area, they may not see the forest for the trees, yet a group of novices can make fundamental mistakes. The amount of expertise required for a group to be effective depends on the purpose of the team. If the purpose is to make incremental, small-scale change, then weighting the team with experts is probably the best strategy. If, on the other hand, the purpose is fundamental, large-scale change (re-engineering), loading the group with individuals with less experience is more appropriate. Large-scale change will require a broader perspective. Experts may find it difficult to empathize with people who do not share their expertise, experience, or perspective.

Clear charter and purpose

One of the most frustrating experiences for team members is not having a clear team direction or purpose. Without clarity, the team may meander and waffle around and after a few overly long meetings, members stop showing up. Team members, their management, and any other stakeholders should agree on the charter and purpose before the team starts its project-based work. Once this charter has been established, it needs to be communicated clearly to the prospective team members.

The right connections

Not only should team members have some political pull themselves, they would benefit from also having access to more important "movers and shakers" within, and sometimes outside, the organization. These connections could include senior departmental and divisional managers from the functions team that the members originate from and represent. As discussed earlier, reaching out to influential stakeholders is an important boundary-spanning activity. Consequently, managers have a responsibility to facilitate access to these connections.

Achievable, noticeable results

Well-established departments tend to have fixed measures of success with clearly defined KRAs and KPIs. In the same way, reasonably early in their formation, cross-functional teams need to decide what results they expect to achieve. To make this task even more challenging for a newly appointed project team, there may be no established measure of success within the company to draw from. An ad hoc project team, for example, may want to reduce waste, or improve the delivery time of products or services to customers. However, the background information may not have been collected before and the team will have to develop a set of KRAs and KPIs specific to the problem they have been charged to solve. Simply put, a project team should understand from the outset what its primary focus is, and the yardstick by which it will be measured.

Understood and agreed-upon ground rules

These ground rules are the guiding norms for the team: for example, issues such as how conflict and consensus can be handled, who writes the minutes and facilitates team meetings, and the degree of formality in those meetings. Other practical issues also need to be addressed by the project team. For instance, how much time, money, and how many people will be available for the project? Who can the group turn to when it needs advice and support? If management fails to follow through on promises, how will the team resolve this? These agreed-upon ground rules will help in managing boundaries early in the life of the project team.

Intensive team-building upfront

Often, a team comes together with good intentions but, due to personal misunderstandings between team members, the team begins to unravel. Typically, consultants are then called in to fix the problem after the damage has been done. It is always better to prevent a problem from happening than to commit to damage control. Upfront team-building sessions, where members' concerns, problems, and issues can be aired, are a constructive way of preventing problems arising through misunderstandings later on in the life of the project. These sessions can also deal with many of the issues described above. These team-building sessions are especially important in cross-functional teams, otherwise it is quite possible that entrenched department rivalries and personality clashes detract from the quality of cross-functional work.

Such team-building sessions serve two important purposes. The first purpose is to train the team in using various tools and approaches to resolve the organizational issues they have been formed to deal with in the first place. These techniques may include such things as problem solving, statistical process control, and flowcharting. After an initial overview, this training is best delivered in a "just in time" fashion, where trainers teach the members the specific tool just before they use it. For example, a team might receive a general overview of techniques in problem solving as part of their initial team building, but specifically learn to process map just before the team needs to apply it to a work problem.

The second purpose of team building involves some training in the usual set of group interaction skills such as meeting management, stages of group development, avoiding groupthink, and communication. There are a variety of strategies to use for rewarding project-based work.

Another important issue is to reinforce positive cross-functional team work through rewards and recognition.

How can teamwork be rewarded?

Broadly, there are two types of rewards for teamwork: monetary and recognition. Below I list some of the ways these rewards can be administered by management.

Monetary rewards

There are several issues that need to be considered when implementing gainsharing reward structures. Gainsharing programs allow team members to "share the gains" of efforts made by a particular team.

This therefore establishes an incentive to help co-workers achieve their shared goals. Three of the most common challenges in applying a gainsharing program are:

- difficulty in measuring precise cost savings or productivity gains;
- inability of team members to see the relationship between the performance of their team and the reward; and
- consideration of whether to reward people who provide essential support and service to the team but who may not directly have contributed to the gain.

It is important for managers to be aware of these challenges when implementing a gainsharing program.

For gainsharing to be effective, rewards must be directly related to team performance so that, if the team succeeds, all members will be rewarded for their contribution. Below are three of the most common forms of monetary rewards for team performance. These are:

- knowledge-based pay;
- one-time bonuses; and
- team incentive system.

Knowledge-based pay

Knowledge-based pay encourages staff to learn new skills and acquire knowledge about the jobs of other team members, by offering incremental pay increases after the new skill is acquired. This method encourages collaboration among team members and facilitates process improvement, since team members can perform many tasks and can understand how the total process works. Knowledge-based pay systems allow the company to support the concept of team learning, while at the same time recognizing outstanding individual performance. Behind this form of incentive is the assumption that the mastery of new skills will ultimately lead to improvements in organizational productivity. Knowledge-based pay systems have a direct application for the facilitation of flexible deployment (see more on flexible deployment in Chapter 5).

One-time bonuses

One-time bonuses can be offered to an ad hoc project team, formed for a specific purpose, that delivers goods or services on time (or ahead of schedule), achieves results under budget, or produces cost-saving ideas. As an illustration, Honeywell's Space Systems Group had a chance to win a major contract for highly specialized computer chips, if it could design the best chip first. Intent on turning out perfect chips with reduced design time, the project manager implemented a "bounty system." He offered each engineer $150 if a chip passed the first design step on time, and up to $1,200 when three chips passed in one design cycle. The team could receive up to $4,000 for similar passes. The team designed two perfect chips in the first cycle, putting Honeywell nine months ahead of its competition.

Team incentive system

The team incentive system is an ongoing reward system (as distinct from the one-time bonus system). For example, cross-functional teams that shorten the time needed to bring new products to market may be paid a bonus by the company on more than one occasion. It is important that the team incentive and the performance target are negotiated upfront between management and the team.

These are some of the more common and successful gainsharing monetary approaches available for teams.

What about non-monetary rewards through recognition?

So far we have discussed reward programs that are tied to specific team outcomes. But it is also possible—and often desirable—to reward cross-functional teams for an unplanned or extraordinary effort. But who and what should be recognized?

There are three dimensions in recognizing performance to consider. The first dimension concerns where the recognition comes from. For instance, some people appreciate recognition from a senior person within the organization, while others value acknowledgment by colleagues and fellow team members.

Another dimension is public or private recognition. Some employees appreciate public rewards, such as having their efforts being recognized in the company newsletter, while others prefer a more personal form of recognition, such as receiving a handwritten note from their boss.

The third dimension in recognizing performance is whether the recognition is intrinsic or extrinsic. Extrinsic motivators are quite different from intrinsic motivators. Extrinsic rewards are positively valued work outcomes that the team or individual receives from some other person in the work setting. For example, recognition in a company newsletter or on a bulletin board by a manager is a form of extrinsic reward. Intrinsic rewards are positively valued work outcomes that the team or individual receives directly, such as the opportunity to take on a challenging assignment. All the evidence suggests that people appreciate recognition, but prefer different forms of recognition.

Here are some practical and effective extrinsic ideas for recognizing teams:

- giving verbal praise at staff meetings;
- inviting the team to present its work at a company conference;
- prominently displaying a poster showing team photographs and accomplishments;
- sending the team on an outing, such as a boat ride or to a sporting event;

- inviting the team to the CEO's home for a barbecue;
- placing a photograph and story about the team in the company or community newspaper;
- encouraging team members to attend professional conferences by paying travel expenses;
- asking the CEO to attend a team meeting to praise its performance;
- sending a letter to the CEO detailing the team's work; and
- giving each team member a T-shirt, hat, or mug with his/her name (or the team's name) on it.

On the other hand, some people respond to intrinsic rewards. Some simple and effective examples include:

- asking the team to accept a new challenge;
- writing timely, thoughtful comments in the margin of the team's reports;
- giving the team the opportunity to meet off-site;
- giving the team improved resources, such as new equipment;
- asking the team's opinion about how to handle problems or new business opportunities;
- asking the team to help another team start up or solve a problem;
- offering to pitch in and help the team directly; and
- empowering the team to act independently.

Both extrinsic and intrinsic rewards are effective in rewarding and reinforcing exceptional team performance. Their value will depend on the team's preference, the culture of the organization, and the resources at the disposal of managers. A combination is often the most effective form of recognition.

From the organization's perspective, the appropriate response to instilling the value of project-based work is to focus on projects, rather than organizational functions. Evidence of this includes promoting, supporting, and encouraging the reconfiguring of psychological boundaries at the cross-functional team level, and de-emphasizing traditional functional boundaries. In a shared sense, employees need to accept and embrace themselves as project-based workers rather than functional-based employees. Evidence of this is a readiness and preparedness to engage in boundary activities at the cross-functional team level rather than building their team identity in the functional department. These individual and organizational mindsets are likely to be characteristic of an organizational culture that has moved from a value of functional-based to a value of project-based work.

The **10** Key Points ...

1. The functionally-based organizational structure is generally pretty inflexible and slow to change direction. It is unsuitable for the twenty-first century.

2. Project-based work can be organized in two ways: temporary or ongoing project teams.

3. The evolution of the network organization is a response to the drivers of change, including heightened competition arising from a globalized marketplace, the transition from a production-based to service-based economy, and the shift to a service orientation.

4. Research has identified three types of boundary activities: buffering, spanning, and bringing up boundaries.

5. It is misguided for organizational leaders to assume that transforming from a traditional bureaucratic to a network organization abolishes psychological boundaries altogether.

6. Six important issues need to be addressed by managers and team members to maximize cross-functional teamwork: proper project team membership; a clear charter and purpose; the right connections; achievable, noticeable results; understood and agreed ground rules; and intensive team-building upfront.

7. There are two types of rewards for teamwork: monetary and recognition.

8. The most common forms of monetary rewards for team performance are knowledge-based pay, one-time bonuses, and team incentive systems.

9. Extrinsic rewards are positively valued work outcomes that the team or individual receives from some other person in the work setting.

10. Intrinsic rewards are positively valued work outcomes that the team or individual receives directly, such the opportunity to take on a challenging assignment.

9

Engaging Hearts and Minds

From human dispirit and work to human spirit and work

> *Heightened expectations of work and the changing nature of the role work plays in people's lives creates a more significant connection between human spirit and work.*

Jeremy, the human resources manager of a large travel agency, was amazed at the variety of ways in which travel agents found a sense of meaning in their daily work.

He was reading through the results of an anonymous survey carried out by an external consultant specializing in employee engagement. Jeremy knew that a minority of staff got little or no meaning from their work with the company. But those who did derive meaning from their work got it from many sources. Jeremy picked out four themes from the survey responses.

Several team members indicated that meaning for them in their work came from the pleasure of assisting their customers to have a memorable travel experience. Jeremy read the responses with interest. One employee said that "sending someone on their holiday, their honeymoon, it's a good feeling." Another person said something similar:

> *You are giving the people their dreams, they may only do one or two big trips away in their life and whether that is going as far as Sydney for the first time or getting on a plane for the first time, or doing that grand tour*

of Europe or Africa, you're giving people their dreams and at the end of the day it comes down to what you do that has a direct influence on how they are going to enjoy their holiday.

Jeremy read another response: "We do say that they're selling people's dreams; you know they're out there helping people live their dream and opening the world to people."

Apart from the idea of selling people's dreams, another theme Jeremy came across as a way employees derived meaning from their work was personal growth. One person said in the report that, when they started working with the company, they knew "nothing about business, and when I eventually leave to work somewhere else I know that I have developed and grown as a person and the company has given me a lot more skills to go out into the world than what I walked in with."

In a similar way, another middle manager said: "There are people who enjoy what they are doing and, especially as you go up the ladder, you get to enjoy it more because you have more control over what you're doing and where you're going."

Another theme Jeremy noticed in the report was based on the benefits employees gained from working with the company. One employee said:

> If you are really, really good you can make some decent money but I think it's more the other benefits of the role, [such as] the opportunity to travel. The company is very good … it gives you the opportunity to purchase shares, it has areas that can help you get healthy. They have financial advisers; they have people that can help you get home loans.

Yet another theme Jeremy identified from the report was the respect employees gained from colleagues in the organization and outside the travel industry. One participant said:

> The organization creates a real community in the sense of you're always interested in how other people are performing, and people do

generally find meaning in their work, and that the longer someone stays the more meaning they find in what they're doing; especially when they feel a sense of accomplishment that they've achieved something.

Apart from admiration from internal colleagues, other employees conceptualized meaning in their work as social status. For example: "Meaning for me is respect from colleagues, respect for myself for what I do, and also respect for just going out socially and meeting people and saying this is what I do." A branch manager emphasized the value he placed on social status by saying that "if you're at a party and someone asks what you do and you say 'I'm a branch manager of a travel agency' it just doesn't gel with anyone. I guess travel doesn't have much respect."

Jeremy sat back in his chair and thoughtfully looked out the window. The way people find meaning in their work is complex, he thought.

Younger employees (aged under 30, in particular) are looking for meaning from their work. Managers who are conscious of this and provide meaningful work, wherever possible, will fulfill this growing need. Older employees or baby boomers, on the contrary, were generally brought up with the notion that work is work, whether it has meaning for them or not. So, when given a job to do they would get on with the work, irrespective of whether or not they derived a sense of meaning from it. Meaning was a secondary consideration to carrying out the work itself. The need for meaningful work was less important than it is today.

So, the value has shifted from human dispirit and work to human spirit and work. This change has come about thanks to several trends in society. For starters, employees want more engagement in their working life because of a general decline in personal connectivity in their surrounding communities. These days the workplace takes center stage as the primary source of community for many people; there has been a general decline in Western society of involvement in neighborhood groups, churches, civic groups, and extended families.

Organizational restructuring in the form of downsizing, re-engineering, and layoffs over the past thirty years has turned the workplace into an environment where employees often feel demoralized and where there is a growing inequality in wages. This places pressure on companies to redress the sense of growing alienation felt by many employees.

The rise in popularity and awareness of Eastern philosophies in the West has encouraged Westerners to look at alternative forms of spirituality. There is an increasing curiosity about Eastern philosophies. Philosophies such as Zen Buddhism and Confucianism, which encourage meditation and stress values such as loyalty to one's groups and discovering one's spiritual center in any activity, are finding greater acceptance. So work is becoming another source of discovering one's spiritual center.

As baby boomers grow closer to retirement, the meaning of life comes into sharper focus. Older workers begin to ask: What is the meaning of life? What does my life mean? Thus, obtaining meaning from everything, including their work, is more important for people moving towards retirement.

Global competition has shifted the focus from technical to human resources. The pressure of global competition has led organizational leaders to recognize that employees' creative energies need a fuller expression at work as a way of combining "head and heart" as a potential competitive advantage.

All of these changes in society have played a part in creating a closer link between work and the human spirit.

From an employee's perspective, work increasingly defines their self-esteem and connection to others. Yet, accelerated change and uncertainty are turning work from something that was once considered stable and predictable into a source of profound insecurity. People are now changing jobs more frequently and the workforce is becoming increasingly fragmented. So, on the one hand, people want more meaning from their work for the variety of reasons mentioned. But, on the other hand, employees are being told there is no guarantee of a long-term job. These are confusing signals. Even though several trends in society have elevated the importance of the value of human spirit and work, it does raise considerable challenges for employees and employers and their respective need to seek and provide meaningful work.

For these reasons, pressure is brought to bear on organizations to fulfill this need for work to be meaningful. Engaging employees is now an important preoccupation. Managers are paying more and more attention to engaging their employees in meaningful work. Of course, a lot of work is routine and mundane and holds little meaning. Endless and pointless meetings, mindless reports, and unquestioningly following processes and procedures fill up a significant part of the work day for most people. But not all work is meaningless—and leaders have the opportunity to engage their workforce in other ways.

Employees, too, have a role to play. It is their responsibility to find work that is meaningful to them. Younger employees, in particular, will tend to sample different jobs until they find something that fulfills them personally. It is likely that a person leaving school today will have nine different vocations in their careers, and this may include a period of being self-employed. The value of human spirit and work is ultimately the joint responsibility of employees and employers.

A recent poll of 14,000 employees across ten European countries by consultants Watson Wyatt has confirmed what a number of similar large-scale surveys have suggested over the past few years: namely, that there is a vast reserve of untapped potential in the workplace in the form of uncommitted or actively disgruntled staff. It also revealed that more than four out of ten employees are actively considering leaving their current employer. While a 2007 poll of almost 90,000 workers by workplace consultancy Towers Perrin found that just 20 percent felt engaged with their work, Watson Wyatt found that only 13 percent (fewer than one in seven) of employees both displayed strong commitment and had a good understanding of the part they could play in making their organizations successful. Only 13 percent of the workforce is fully engaged and trying to create value for their organization. What are the other 87 percent of the workforce doing?[1]

---

[1] Brown, E.D. (2008) Employee engagement – Not just a buzzword! At http://ericbrown.com/employee-engagement-not-just-a-buzzword.htm, accessed January 2014.

What exactly does "human spirit and work" mean?

The quest to find meaning in work is not new. Many writers have, over a long period of time, written about the importance of job satisfaction and employee happiness for individuals and organizations alike. Some surveys indicate that many employees across a lot of industries consider their work dissatisfying and an unhappy experience, to the extent that some think their work experience wounds their human spirit. For the reasons I mentioned earlier, the importance of finding meaning in work is more important now than ever before.

It is important to clarify that spirituality at work has nothing to do with being converted to a new religion, or getting people to accept a basic belief system. It is about employees having their spiritual needs nourished through their work. Spirituality at work has to do with employees experiencing a sense of purpose and meaning in their work. This idea of fulfillment has a bearing on a person's self-esteem. It goes beyond finding meaning in the performance of work-related tasks. Spirituality at work is concerned with the connection between a person's work and their human spirit. It is also about people experiencing a sense of connectedness to one another and to their workplace community. Business leaders also recognize that nourishing an individual's spirit at work may be good for business; it may help them be more engaged in their work.

What conditions are necessary for employees to experience well-being at work?

For a growing number of people, work is no longer simply a source of income, but also an important factor in generating and maintaining personal growth, and a source of well-being. A job that provides only income, but no recognition, no learning, no compatibility with the rest of the social environment, is a job that cannot do much to enhance the well-being of the contemporary employee beyond paying the bills.

General well-being in work is associated with an employee's working environment, their role in the production process, and the social significance of work.

Let us look briefly at each of these three factors.

Working environment

The foundation for the quality of working conditions is efficiency and justice in the allocation of resources. In particular, employees' perception of their immediate manager's trust in them can affect their job satisfaction. People's sense of fairness and equity at work will play an important factor in their well-being.

Role in production process

Producing the organization's goods and services and the role that employees play in that process has a huge bearing on their welfare. If people feel their work role is significant in generating productivity, this is likely to have a positive impact on their well-being. On the other hand, if they feel no connection with the organization's productivity through their job, employees are more likely to see their work as insignificant and will most likely withdraw and disengage.

Social significance of work

The social significance of work is becoming increasingly important. Work and the way it fits in with, and serves, other social activities contributes to meaning beyond financial rewards. Having friends in the workplace and feeling a sense of community is becoming an increasingly important factor for people's sense of well-being.

Heightened expectations of work and the changing nature of the role work plays in people's lives have created a more significant connection between the concept of human spirit and work. It is more important now for managers to understand the specific conditions necessary for fostering well-being at work. This means maintaining working conditions that are safe and pleasant, and creating jobs that contribute to individual and social well-being.

How do people construct meaning in their work?

According to Jesper Isaksen's research, employees gain meaning from work on three distinct levels.[2] Let's look at each level so that we can better understand how people derive meaning from work.

Level 1: Role of work

The first level concerns the general meaning of work. What role does work play in creating meaning for me in my life? Some people work to live and others live to work. Our expectations of the role work plays in our lives come from our early experiences, listening to what our parents said about work around the dining room table. Organizations understandably have very little influence on this first level.

Level 2: Role of a specific type of work

The second level concerns the general meaning in a specific type of work. For example, what is the meaning of being a nurse? People are attracted to particular kinds of work for a variety of reasons. People's attraction to a certain type of work is often based on the degree to which that kind of work is aligned with their values. For instance, a person may be attracted to nursing because they get a sense of fulfillment from helping others in need. Here, again, organizations have little influence over this second level.

Level 3: Role of a specific job

The third level is the personal meaning associated with work. For example, do you find your current work as a nurse meaningful? The general and personal meanings of work in the second and

---

[2] Isaksen, J. (2000) "Constructing meaning despite the drudgery of repetitive work." *Journal of Humanistic Psychology* 40(3), 84–107.

third levels do not necessarily have the same content or depth. To illustrate what I mean, a nurse may find the nursing profession meaningful as such (level 2), and, at the same time, find her own job as a nurse (level 3) absolutely meaningless because of the demands her particular job places on her. This level of meaning (or lack of) is directly related to the job the person is currently doing. Broadly speaking, people bring to an organization a general idea about their vocation and through their interaction with their working environment their day-to-day work develops a personal meaning to them. Organizations definitely can influence the degree of meaning employees gain (or don't gain) from their organizational work.

AT THE COALFACE . . .

Jesper Isaksen researched employees performing highly repetitive and mundane work in a particular catering company, using three criteria: (1) meaning through attachment to the workplace and its procedures, (2) meaning through engagement with their work colleagues, (3) meaning based on the concept of work being a necessary part of life. He found that "meaningful" and "meaningless" are not simply outcomes of some specific working conditions. The construction of meaning was the result of workers' spontaneous and continuous effort and will, and was shaped by employees regardless of the kinds of workplace conditions they had to endure. All twenty-eight employees in Isaksen's sample faced the same hindrances in their work, and had more or less the same type of repetitive work. Despite these obstacles, some still experienced work as meaningful overall, whereas others did not.[3]

---

[3] Isaksen, J. (2000) "Constructing Meaning despite the Drudgery of Repetitive Work." *Journal of Humanistic Psychology* 40(3), 84–107.

Based on Isaksen's meaningful work construct, the provision of adequate working conditions in a company cannot guarantee that staff will find their work meaningful. Apart from this research, I have come across no studies that support a direct relationship between satisfactory working conditions and the creation of stimulating and meaningful work. Despite this apparent lack of evidence, it is a common misconception among managers that good working conditions can positively influence the motivation of their workforce. This raises some questions: Does this mean that companies should not bother making their organizations more attractive places to work? Will employees generate their own meaning about their jobs, independent of their working conditions?

Before managers start slashing their budgets, they should consider this: poor working conditions will create a level of frustration within the workforce. And this level of irritation will most likely lower the number of people in the organization who actually experience meaning in their work. In other words, people who have very few and narrow work interests when they start their job are most probably going to become disenchanted in their personal efforts to create meaning if the company provides poor working conditions. Poor working conditions limit the potential for some employees to develop meaning through their specific job. If individuals have low expectations of the likelihood of constructing meaning in any job beforehand, they will tend to experience even greater difficulty obtaining it in a working environment that is rigid and lacks stimulation. It is for this reason that managers need to provide stimulating work environments.

As we have discussed, the degree of fit between individual and organization depends partly on the aspirations for meaning the individual brings to the job they do. But just as important is the degree of help or hindrance the organization provides in the working climate and conditions. In broad terms, meaning in work is derived from the interaction between employees and their workplace. It is therefore important for managers to understand that meaningfulness is not an inherent characteristic of a specific type of work or a place of work. It is in fact a subjective judgment made by employees in their association with their workplace.

Both the conditions of the workplace and personal characteristics of the employee have to be considered to understand why some people construct meaning, whereas others do not. Some people have personality traits that predispose them towards easily constructing meaning, whereas other people have personal characteristics that make it difficult for them to construct meaning in some or all types of work. Likewise, some workplaces offer optimal working conditions that facilitate the creation of meaning, while other workplaces offer poor working conditions that hinder the development of meaning.

What are the elements of human spirit and work?

Managers should be aware that if they fail to meet their responsibilities they will inhibit the potential for employees to find the work they do meaningful. Meaningful work can be repressed in three ways: poor working conditions, poor fit between employee interests and job opportunities, and lack of belief by managers in their capacity to provide employees with meaning in their work.

It is therefore important for managers to address these three elements. Managers ought to ask themselves: What can I do to improve the working conditions, match employees' interests with the work that needs doing, and find ways for employees to discover meaning in their daily work? If these issues are neglected by an organization, the potential for the human spirit to be nourished in that workplace is diminished considerably.

As with the other seven values in the New Employment Relationship Model, the value of human spirit and work is the mutual responsibility of the employer and employee. The three elements of moving from a value of human dispirit and work to a value of human spirit and work are:

- the provision of good working conditions by the employer and a willingness to appreciate these good working conditions by the employee;
- wherever possible, managers look for ways for employees to find meaning in their daily work and, reciprocally, employees ought to display the capacity to find personal meaning in their daily work; and
- an obligation by managers to coordinate the interests of employees with the work that needs doing should be matched by employees' willingness to seek out work that corresponds with their interests.

Operating from a traditional mindset, is it possible for managers to misuse this knowledge to exploit workers? In other words, just give employees a sense of meaningfulness and then exploit them in other ways; for example, by reducing wages and at the same time expecting the worker to take on more responsibility? I don't think this will work. Employees quickly sense exploitation and this will no doubt lead to a negative perception of the working environment, and a mismatch between the person and their working environment. Taking advantage of employees in this way will be self-defeating.

On the other hand, an organization that improves its working conditions to genuinely support employees' efforts to find their work meaningful will recoup their investment. This authentic attempt by management is likely to pay off in terms of higher levels of job fulfillment and employee engagement than otherwise would be the case.

Employees have obligations too. It is ultimately employees' responsibility to find work that is stimulating and meaningful. As author David Noer eloquently puts it, "there is power, excitement, and amazing productivity when our work is congruent with our personal mission and values."[4] If people seek out work that nourishes their human spirit and organizations reciprocate by offering employees opportunities to participate in meaningful, stimulating tasks and projects, it can create enormous advantages for individuals and organizations. "If organizations can provide the spark that ignites employees' reservoir of human spirit and allow people to apply it to work that they perceive as meaningful, the organization has unleashed a powerful competitive weapon of creative energy" (Noer 1997). An important factor associated in creating a connection between human spirit and organizational work is a degree of flexibility, optimism, and creativity in matching organizational work to the individual's strengths and interests.

What does it mean for an employee to be fully engaged?

I define engagement as the extent to which people make the connection between their human spirit and the work they do. It is different to commitment. The concept of commitment will be covered extensively in Chapter 10. For more than thirty years, managers have been wrestling with the organizational factors that engage (or disengage) employees. Researchers have also been conducting studies to determine the link between an engaged workforce and organizational performance. While some research remains inconclusive, there is a growing body of work that associates employee engagement with organizational performance.

---

[4] Noer, D.M. (1997) *Breaking Free: A Prescription for Personal and Organizational Change*. San Francisco: Jossey-Bass.

This is evidenced by research that found employees who responded more favorably to survey questions on engagement, also worked in business units with higher levels of productivity, profit, retention, and customer satisfaction. It is also significant that the manager—not the remuneration or benefits—was the key to building and sustaining an engaged workforce.

Before I explain how organizational leaders can put into practice a strategy for employee engagement, it would be helpful to define what *engaged employee* means and how this differs from *disengaged employee*. Fully engaged employees:

- demonstrate more enthusiasm and use that enthusiasm to achieve the organization's mission and goals;
- are less likely to leave for other employment opportunities, because they enjoy what they are doing and find their work meaningful;
- like their work environment and the people they work with;
- tell others about the organization and are more likely to refer good employment candidates;
- have a sense of pride and ownership in what they do within the organization; and
- are more productive and contribute more significantly to the organization's success.

Most of us can identify an engaged employee, but these descriptions may help.

Disengaged employees, on the other hand, are more likely to be costly to the organization. For instance, disengaged employees are absent from work more frequently and for longer periods of time. They are less productive on average and therefore more of a liability to the company. While it is difficult to quantify the cost of disengaged employees, it is likely that they have a significantly negative impact on quality, safety, customer satisfaction, and missed opportunities in increased productivity. The vast majority of employees could be classified as falling between these two extreme definitions of engagement and disengagement.

How do I put into practice an employment engagement strategy?

One way to foster the value of human spirit and work in a workplace is the implementation of an employee engagement strategy. To apply this strategy, the first step is to measure the overall current level of engagement within the company. Reputable employee engagement surveys can be a good tool for measuring the level of engagement of employees in an organization. These kinds of surveys serve several useful purposes:

- They communicate the right values.
- They provide the organization with useful data.
- They can be used as benchmarking tools to monitor engagement over an extended period of time.

Let's look at these three benefits in more detail.

Communication of values

The kind of surveys adopted by management communicates to the workforce the values that are considered important in that particular company. Employee engagement surveys signal to the workforce the importance and relevance of capturing the hearts and minds of people in their organization.

Useful data

Well-constructed and administered surveys have the potential to provide useful data. Employee engagement surveys can provide information to help employers understand the level of engagement between employees and the company. This information can be used to put in place strategies to improve employee commitment.

Benchmarking

Apart from being a useful source of data, survey results provide organizations with benchmarks, which can be used to monitor annual progress towards predetermined goals. Externally, benchmarks provide baseline, historic, and normative contrast so that the organization can be compared with other organizations within and outside their particular industry.

If done thoroughly, these three benefits provide a useful reason for implementing an engagement survey. However, it is important to note that employee surveys, no matter how well crafted, do not in themselves create fully engaged employees. Effective feedback, action planning, implementation, and follow-up of the survey results are the critical steps in formulating and executing an employment engagement strategy. By collecting survey data from an organizational setting, there is a heightened expectation from survey participants that something constructive will be done with the results. If nothing is done, then cynicism sets in. But, done properly, survey results can be a catalyst for change and organizational development.

The use of employee surveys as a management tool has significantly increased over the past fifty years. While most organizations are likely to see the value of implementing an employee survey process, many companies fail to obtain significant and sustainable value from surveying their staff. This is usually because they do not follow through on the data collected.

It is important that all members of the organization are given the opportunity to participate in the survey. Apart from comparing horizontal engagement levels across functions or departments, the survey should also be structured to compare the vertical perspectives of the three organizational strata: top management, middle management, and workforce. This vertical analysis can lead to many useful insights, and these understandings will not be picked up in a horizontal analysis. For example, top management may collectively hold the view that employees are given ample opportunity to grow and develop. However, the workforce perspective could collectively hold the opposite view, and the middle management perspective may be split on this issue. This kind of result should be a wake-up call to top management that their growth and development strategies are not being perceived positively by the group they are intended for—the workforce. Therefore, by stratifying the organization, survey results can be compared horizontally (between functions) and vertically (between organizational layers) to yield better results.

What do we do with the survey results?

Action planning is the critical practical component of any survey process. Without following through and implementing action plans, managers fall short of identifying important opportunities to improve the overall health of the workforce. Some managers do not know what to do with the survey results, do not understand where to start, or how to identify important priorities for action planning, while others get snowed under by other priorities—which signals to employees that other things are more important or, worse still, that the survey was not important and employees' opinions don't count for much.

What is an employee engagement strategy?

An employee engagement strategy really starts once the results of the survey are known. An action plan starts with categorizing survey items based on different levels of employee engagement, both horizontally and vertically. There are various levels of engagement. I have defined these levels (or tiers) of engagement based on well-founded motivational theories that suggest that certain factors need to be met before employees can achieve a level of meaning in their work.

I have divided engagement items into three progressive tiers, each tier addressing higher individual and organizational needs. Well-established models of human functioning and employee motivation, such as Abraham Maslow's *hierarchical theory of needs* (physiological, safety, belonging, esteem, and self-actualization), Clayton Alderfer's *ERG model* (existence, relatedness, and growth), and Frederick Herzberg's *two-factor theory* (hygiene and motivators) form the basis for making sense of the data from a employee engagement survey.[5] All three theoretical models describe different levels of fulfillment, starting with basic or "necessary for survival" needs. While my Employee Engagement Strategy Model (see Figure 9.1) does not directly mirror these theorists' ideas, it does apply the same principle of a hierarchical structure and the need for engagement along different dimensions.

Explanations of the three dimensions (basic, intermediate, and advanced) of employee engagement in Figure 9.1 are outlined below.

Basic engagement needs: working conditions

The first tier is the category that addresses needs in a job to enable a basic level of engagement. These basic needs are the starting point for an organization to play its role in instilling the value of human spirit and work from an organizational perspective. Basic items are fundamental to any reasonable job in an organization, and range from safe working conditions to being treated fairly. Most employees take these basic engagement issues for granted; however, if left unmet or unfulfilled; employees are likely to become fundamentally dispirited with their work.

---

[5] Wood, J. et al. (2013) *Organisational Behaviour: Core Concepts and Applications*, 3rd Australasian edition. Milton, Queensland: John Wiley & Sons.

Advanced Needs – Organizational Obligations

Customer focus, organizational growth and success belief in competitive strategy, product and service improvement, confidence in top management

Intermediate Needs – Growth and Development

Learning and performance development, encouragement, sense of belonging, cooperation between teams, personal growth and fulfillment, adequate pay and benefits, open communication channels, pride in products and services

Basic Needs – Working Conditions

Safe working conditions, good teamwork, competent supervisor (setting goals, coaching, feedback, recognition), adequate tools and equipment, basic skills training, fair treatment

FIG 9.1 / The Employee Engagement Strategy Model[6]

Basic engagement factors provide a solid foundation for action planning. Organizational leaders can use the results of their employee survey to work on established survey dimensions such as quality, job satisfaction, environment, health and safety, communications, and management practices.

Intermediate engagement needs: growth and development

The second tier is the category that addresses the growth and development needs of the individual. These items make up the intermediate category of engagement. Once the basics have been

---

[6] Baker, T.B. (2009) *The 8 Values of Highly Productive Companies: Creating Wealth from a New Employment Relationship*. Brisbane: Australian Academic Press.

met, employees are likely to focus on these intermediate factors. They range from learning and performance development to pride in the company's products and services. If intermediate factors are fulfilled, employees' engagement with their work and the company has the potential to improve beyond the basic level.

The value of human spirit and work is therefore likely to be more deeply embedded within the culture of the organization once the growth and development needs of the individual have been identified and fulfilled.

Advanced engagement needs: organizational obligation

The third tier is the category that addresses organizational obligation needs. These items make up the advanced engagement category. To exceed employees' expectations of gaining meaning from their work, advanced factors need to be addressed. They range from customer focus to confidence in top management. An important distinction between the first two tiers and the advanced tier is the focus of the employee. In the basic and intermediate needs, the focus is on the individual and his/her welfare. These needs are fundamental to all jobs and the growth and development of the individual as a person and employee. The advanced needs, on the other hand, are focused on external factors such as the customer and the employee's relationship with the organization as a whole.

For employees to be optimally engaged, external factors beyond the person cannot be ignored. More specifically, the employee's professional relationship with the customer and top management is likely to have a significant bearing on the extent to which s/he finds meaning in the working environment. For instance, it is very unlikely that a person can be fully engaged in their work if they dislike dealing with their customers and mistrust management.

While this employee engagement strategy follows the hierarchical structure of reputable theories of motivation, one level does not necessarily need to be completely fulfilled before moving on to the next level. It simply identifies three tiers of employee engagement. However, in order to improve employee engagement, managers should first look to the basic items and, if low scores or deficiencies are evident, begin working on those items. For instance, demonstrating how much a company is doing for a community cause (advanced item) is fine, but it will not help to engage employees if their work equipment does not function properly or if the employee does not feel valued and respected by his/her supervisor. Eventually a deficiency in the basic tier will probably mean that employees will either leave the company or retreat in some other way, such as decreasing their productivity or increasing their absenteeism. So, it makes sense to start with the basic tier needs first.

The use of the three tiers of employee engagement assists an organization in arranging its priorities in terms of employee engagement. Therefore, low scores on basic items should receive a higher priority for action planning. Action plans to counter low scores on intermediate issues should be dealt with once basic items have been addressed.

Advanced items ought to be dealt with once basic and intermediate items have been addressed. Companies with fully engaged employees devote time and resources to improving the items in the advanced tier because most of the items in the basic and intermediate tiers have already been fulfilled. Consequently, this tiered approach I advocate is a convenient way for managers to prioritize their employees' and organizational needs around the value of human spirit and work.

Another common error managers make is to use a top-down approach to address issues arising from survey results. Instead, I would suggest creating a project team to analyze the data and make the necessary recommendations. As discussed in Chapter 8, a project-based team should be a cross-functional team that is reasonably representative of the organization at large. This team will then be given the important role of advancing the value of human spirit and work from an organizational perspective. Its methodology is based on a bottom-up rather than top-down approach. It is likely therefore that those employees will feel a greater sense of ownership and commitment to their recommended strategies. As the old saying goes, people don't argue with their own data. (If you would like a copy of the engagement survey, then please go to www.winnersatwork.com.au.).

From the organization's perspective, the appropriate response to instilling the value of human spirit and work is to focus on providing work that is meaningful, wherever possible. Evidence of this includes providing good working conditions, creating the right fit between employees' interests and job opportunities, and giving them the chance to construct meaning from their daily work. It is ultimately the responsibility of the employee to find work that is meaningful. More specifically, employees are accountable for appreciating good working conditions when and where they exist, a willingness to look for meaning in their daily work, and a readiness to apply their interests to the job at hand. These individual and organizational mindsets are features of an organizational culture that has moved from a value of human dispirit and work to a value of human spirit and work.

The **10** Key Points ...

1. The value has shifted from human dispirit and work to human spirit and work. This change has come about because of several trends in society.

2. Work increasingly defines many employees' self-esteem and connection to others.

3. It is important to clarify that spirituality at work has nothing to do with religion, or getting people to accept a basic belief

system. It is about employees having their spiritual needs nourished through their work.

4. General well-being in work is associated with an employee's work environment, their role in the production process, and the social significance of work.

5. Broadly speaking, people bring to an organization a general idea about their vocation and through their interaction with a work environment develop personal meaning in their day-to-day work.

6. Meaningful work can be repressed in three ways: poor working conditions, poor fit between employee interests and job opportunities, and lack of belief from managers in their capacity to provide employees with meaningful work.

7. Engagement is defined as the extent to which people make the connection between their human spirit and the work they do. It is different from commitment.

8. One way to foster the value of human spirit and work in a workplace is the implementation of an employee engagement strategy.

9. The Employee Engagement Strategy Model has three tiers: advanced needs (organizational obligations); intermediate needs (growth and development); and basic needs (working conditions).

10. From the organization's perspective, the appropriate response to instilling the value of human spirit and work is to focus on providing work that is meaningful, wherever possible. It is ultimately the responsibility of the employee to find work that is meaningful to them.

chapter 10

Committing to the Cause

From loyalty to commitment

> *Today, employers not only do not expect to work for decades for the same company, they do not necessarily want to.*

"These three employees have demonstrated great loyalty to this company," said Jim. "I think we should reward them at the Christmas party." "What did you have in mind, Jim?" asked Chris, Jim's boss. "I thought we should buy each of them a flat-screen plasma TV and present it at the party. What do you think?" said Jim.

Chris looked at Jim pensively. "What signal will this send the troops, Jim?" inquired Chris.

"It will send a signal to staff that we value them; we care about them. It demonstrates that we value loyalty in our staff," Jim said.

There was a long pause and Chris asked, "What about commitment? Does it show that we value commitment?"

"What do you mean, Chris? Aren't they the same thing—loyalty and commitment?" Jim asked.

"No, I don't think so. You can be loyal without being committed and committed without being loyal," Chris replied.

"What do you mean?"

"You have a university degree, don't you, Jim?"

"Yes, I do," Jim responded.

"Well, you must have shown a level of commitment to complete that qualification, right? But that doesn't necessarily mean you were loyal to the university that issued you your qualification, does it?"

"I guess not," said Jim with a puzzled look.

"Similarly, a university student can be loyal to a partner in a short-term relationship, but that doesn't necessarily mean they will have a long-term commitment for life," Chris continued. "Remember, Jim, the only rats that leave a sinking ship are the ones that can swim. Sometimes we don't want or need people to stay with the company for a long time. It's what people do that is important, not how long people decide to stay."

After another long pause, Jim asked, "Should we be rewarding loyalty or commitment?"

"I'm not against recognizing these three employees for their length of service. But I think we should balance this by recognizing those employees who are committed to assisting our company achieve its business goals," Chris replied.

"Okay, I get your point. I'll rethink this and get back to you," Jim said.

Few business leaders would deny the importance of organizational loyalty, perhaps fewer still believe they can achieve it the way they once did. After all, the lifetime contract between the individual and organization expired long ago. Employees who have embraced the mindset of the new psychological contract are more likely to display loyalty to their careers before their current employer.

The idea of showing loyalty to an organization has all but disappeared, and a good thing too. It is a rare thing nowadays for an employee to display loyalty to one boss throughout their entire career. In the last generation, it wasn't that uncommon to stay with one organization for your entire career. Many older managers I come into contact with bemoan the lack of loyalty these days. The issue of loyalty can be confusing for employers. Employers often think that if an employee is not loyal they are also not committed to the organization. That's simply not true. You can be committed without being loyal.

For example, you can successfully commit to getting fit over a three-month period, but that doesn't necessarily mean that you will be loyal to the gym you attend. Similarly, an employee can work for an organization with total commitment for six months and leave for another opportunity. Just because they leave doesn't mean they weren't committed while they were employed. Alternatively, someone can be loyal without showing commitment. To use the gym example again, that same person could be loyal to the gym for several years, paying their membership fees each year on time but only using its equipment two or three times! Or, as one of my university students put it to me: "It's like dating: You can be faithful to the person you're seeing now while you're involved with him or her, but that doesn't mean you won't move on to dating someone else later." In a similar way, a company should not (and increasingly cannot) strive to keep all its employees forever. Instead of loyalty, modern corporations ought to be cultivating mutual commitment between employer and employee—albeit for a limited timeframe.

In the same way, someone can work for a boss for twenty years, thereby displaying great loyalty, but coast along and never really commit to achieving certain performance standards. Under these circumstances, if you were an employer, who would you want to employ: a committed or a loyal employee? Of course, having an employee who is committed *and* loyal is the best option, but given a choice I would prefer a committed employee.

A binding value of the New Employment Relationship Model is commitment. In the traditional employee–employer relationship an underpinning value was loyalty. In the Traditional Employment Relationship Model, the employee would display loyalty to the organization and, in exchange, they would receive loyalty from the organization in terms of a clearly defined career path and opportunities to build a career. What employers need now is a committed employee who assists them in achieving the goals of the business. Younger employees, in particular, would also prefer a committed employer to a loyal one. For example, if the organization is committed to assisting employees achieve their personal goals, such as balancing their home and work responsibilities through flexible work practices, they are more inclined to feel a sense of commitment or obligation to that employer. It is for this reason that commitment replaces loyalty as a mutual exchange process between employer and employee.

Managers who can practically demonstrate a sense of commitment to assisting employees achieve their personal goals will—in most cases—receive commitment from their employees to achieve organizational performance goals. This means committing to such things as flexible working arrangements and sponsoring opportunities to develop skills that are likely to enhance their careers. This can be done even with the knowledge that the recipient employee may only stay with the employer for a short period of time. Yet, ironically, by committing to these sorts of things, the employee may stay with the organization for a longer period of time than would otherwise be the case. In addition, an employee treated this way may feel an obligation to reciprocate with heightened performance. Whereas loyalty is a more sentimental form of exchange between employer and employee, commitment is a more pragmatic exchange: that is, "you scratch my back and I'll scratch yours."

What is the difference between human spirit and work and commitment?

On the surface, it seems like the value of human spirit and work and a meaningful work construct (discussed in Chapter 9) means the same thing as the value of commitment. Even though there are elements that overlap the two values, human spirit and work and commitment have different emphases. Human spirit and work stresses the relationship between the individual and his/her work and its associated conditions. More broadly, the value of commitment is concerned with the link between the individual and the organization. To illustrate this distinction, an employee may find the job s/he does meaningful (human spirit and work) but still not be committed to the organization's vision (commitment). Conversely, a person can have a sense of commitment to the organization's vision, but not find their job very meaningful. It is in the best interests of individual and organization to cultivate both these values.

Today, employers not only do not expect to work for decades for the same company, but they do not necessarily want to. Progressive-thinking employees are largely disillusioned with the very idea of loyalty to organizations. But, at the same time, they do not really want to shift employers every eighteen months for their entire working life. It would be disruptive and inconvenient. Likewise, organizations don't want to continually experience high staff turnover. Companies would grind to a halt if they had to replace large portions of the workforce every eighteen months. Employers will always require focused and skilled employees. Employees require the capacity to maintain their employability through career development opportunities. These two needs of committed employees and the career development of organizations and employees respectively are not necessarily mutually exclusive. This is especially so when the skills that a person masters to further his/her own career are also what the company needs in the short term to increase its performance.

How can we measure commitment?

The value of commitment is defined as the employee's psychological attachment to the organization. It can be contrasted with other work-related attitudes such as job satisfaction (an employee's feelings about his/her job) and organizational identification (the degree to which employees experience a sense of one-ness with their company). Although they are different concepts, there is some connection between commitment, satisfaction, and identification.

Organizational psychologists have developed many definitions of organizational commitment, and numerous scales to measure it. One example of this work is John Meyer and Natalie Allen's *model of commitment*, which was developed to integrate numerous definitions of commitment that had proliferated in the literature on the subject of organizational commitment.[1] According to them, there are three states of mind that can characterize an employee's commitment to the organization.

Here is a brief summary of each mindset:

Affective commitment (desire)

Affective commitment is defined as the employee's emotional attachment to the organization. Consequently, s/he strongly identifies

---

[1] Meyer, J.P. & Allen, N.J. (1991) "A three-component conceptualization of organisational commitment." *Human Resource Management Review* 1, 61–89.

with the goals of the company and desires to remain a part of the organization. In other words, the employee commits to the organization because s/he "wants to." When firms help employees acquire new skills that support their professional and personal advancement, they can potentially win the commitment from those employees to achieving organizational goals. The transaction is also likely to be attractive to potential employees. Paradoxically, employers can instill a sense of commitment from workers by helping them "grow out" of their jobs, into new ones within the same company, or in another company.

Continuance commitment (cost)

Continuance commitment is defined as the employee's attachment to the organization because of the perceived costs of leaving to work somewhere else. The individual commits to the organization because he/she sees the high personal costs of losing organizational membership, including economic losses (such as superannuation accruals) and social costs (membership ties with co-workers). Simply put, the employee remains with a company because he/she "has to."

Normative commitment (obligation)

Normative commitment is defined as the employee's attachment to an organization due to obligation. The individual commits to and remains with a company because of feelings of indebtedness. For instance, the company may have invested resources in training an employee who then feels a sense of obligation to put more effort into his/her job and stay with the organization to "repay the debt." It may also reflect a personal belief or value, developed before the person joins the organization through family or other means, that one should be loyal to one's organization. In other words, the employee stays with the organization because s/he "ought to."

Meyer and Allen's model shows that the value of commitment can be characterized by three different mindsets: *desire*, *cost* and *obligation*. Employees with a strong affective commitment stay because they want to, those with a strong normative commitment stay because they feel they ought to, and those with a strong continuance commitment stay because they have to.

What are the elements of commitment?

In line with the other seven values in the model, applying the value of commitment is a joint venture between employer and employee. The three key individual mindsets are a desire to acquire organizationally-sponsored professional and personal skills; the perceived cost of leaving the organization; and a sense of obligation to the organization. From the organizational perspective, the appropriate response is a commitment to providing professional and personal skills opportunities, financial and social inducements, and investing resources in developing employees.

These elements of the value of commitment are not mutually exclusive from an employee's point of view: an individual can simultaneously be committed to an organization in an affective, normative, and continuance sense, at varying levels of intensity. At any time, an employee has a "commitment profile" that reflects high or low levels of all three of these mindsets, and different profiles have different effects on workplace behavior, such as job performance, absenteeism, and the chance that they will leave.

Research suggests that employees who want to stay (desire) tend to perform at a higher level than those who do not. Employees who remain out of obligation also tend to outperform those who feel no such obligation, but the effect on performance is not as strong as that observed for desire. Finally, employees who have to stay primarily to avoid losing something of value (cost—e.g., benefits, seniority) often have little incentive to do anything more than what is required to retain their position. So, not all forms of commitment are alike.

What can be done in practice to increase commitment?

Aligning career growth with company goals

Aligning career growth with company goals can be an effective practical way of impacting on affective, normative, and continuance commitment. When a company helps its employees develop expertise that furthers their professional and personal development, employees generally feel a sense of obligation and desire to assist the organization to achieve its outcomes. If the program of study is ongoing, the employee may also perceive a significant cost in leaving before the development program is completed. A properly executed and relevant skills development program has the potential of aligning employee career development and organizational commitment. How does an organization achieve this alignment?

A practical starting point is a genuine discussion between the manager and his/her staff on the employee's career goals. It is also helpful, wherever possible, for managers to assist their people to identify a link between their own professional and personal goals and the company's goals. When people understand the wider business framework in which the company is operating, they can, potentially, more easily define ways to advance their own careers within the context of the organization.

It should also be acknowledged that frank and frequent dialogue about careers can decrease commitment. Employees may part ways with their employer when they discover that they cannot achieve their career goals. However, on balance, honest and regular dialogue between managers and staff is more likely to be beneficial to both the individual and organization.

Some companies use assessment tools and career coaches to identify employees' strengths and decide how to best leverage those talents for the company's good. These companies also encourage employees to initiate conversations about how their strengths and talents might be best used in the organization. When employees are using their strengths, they find their work more satisfying, and feel that they are supporting their own career paths. Aligning career goals with company goals has the potential to positively affect all three elements of commitment.

AT THE COALFACE . . .

A staff accountant at Choctawatchee Electric Cooperative, Inc. (CHELCO), a Florida-based electricity cooperative, benefited from assessment tools and career coaching. When the accountant expressed interest in a management position, her coach reminded her that her assessment indicated strengths in areas other than management. The accountant then acknowledged that her interest in management stemmed primarily from the earning potential of the managerial position. She could not see any other way to increase her earning capacity, apart from leaving to work somewhere else. Based on her interest and commitment to furthering her career, as well as on her educational background and strengths, including attention to detail, and adherence to company policies and procedures, the company offered her the position of revenue analyst. In this new role, she provided more value to the organization and took on new challenges. She also increased her earning potential because the new position was rated several grades higher than her former position as an accountant.[2]

---

[2] Johnson, L.K. (2005) "Rethinking Company Loyalty," in L.A. Hall (ed.), *Working Knowledge: The Thinking That Leads*. Boston, MA: Harvard Business School.

Design work with variety and autonomy

Jobs that offer variety and the scope to make decisions (and even mistakes) can engender commitment from those filling them. Allowing staff to take ownership of projects gives them the opportunity to develop new skills and, just as importantly, the chance to demonstrate what they are capable of. Flexible deployment strategies that promote autonomy could take the form of job rotation, job enrichment, job enlargement, or multi-skilling (see Chapter 5). At the very least, managers need to let employees know how and when they can exercise choice in their work role. As a simple and practical illustration, a public relations firm may use their weekly staff meeting to share responsibility. They can use the meeting to invite expressions of interest from staff to project manage key accounts. By giving staff options in the assignments they undertake, managers are encouraging employees to match their job interests with the work that needs doing.

Focus on relationships

For many people in the workforce, commitment is fostered through good relationships with supervisors and colleagues. Exit interviews suggest that one of the main reasons that people decide to leave a company to work somewhere else is not inadequate pay or benefits; it is more often than not their difficult day-to-day relationship with their immediate superior. Managers would do well to appreciate that positive working relationships with employees is essential for instilling a sense of commitment from employees. Also, fostering supportive relationships among employees in a team or unit can generate a sense of obligation to their work colleagues. Apart from the manager/staff relationships, peer relationships can, and often do, have a major bearing on continuance commitment for employees.

Matching individual and organizational values

The integration of employee and organizational values is another powerful way to increase organizational commitment. A good example of linking staff and organizational values occurs at Medtronic, a medical device developer in Minneapolis. Medtronic broadcasts to its 30,000 employees worldwide stories of patients who have benefited from the company's products. In the words of a senior executive: "Our people end up feeling personally involved in our company's mission to restore people to full life. They can see the end result of their work. Many of them are profoundly moved by the patients' stories."

The matching of personal and organizational values builds affective commitment. By putting a human face on its mission, Medtronic has achieved employee-retention rates above the industry average. The company gets an impressive 95 percent favorable response rate to the employee survey item: "I have a clear understanding of Medtronic's mission" and a 93 percent favorable response to another statement: "The work I do supports the Medtronic mission."[3] Of course, a company's mission is especially compelling when patients' lives are at stake. But companies in any industry can find creative ways to help employees see how their daily work has a personal impact on the lives of their customers. Employees in these circumstances commit to the organization because they "want to."

Work–life balance

Another important area impacting more and more on organizational commitment is addressing the ever-increasing challenges associated with balancing work and home responsibilities. Implementing practical

---

[3] Johnson, L.K. (2005) "Rethinking Company Loyalty," in L.A. Hall (ed.), *Working Knowledge: The Thinking That Leads.* Boston, MA: Harvard Business School.

strategies to help people overcome conflict between work and home is a powerful way for companies to retain their core employees. Career success is less likely to be measured simply in terms of advancement than it used to be. It is only relatively recently that a significant number of employees have begun to define career success in terms of work–home balance rather than climbing the corporate ladder. Some organizations are notable for their genuine efforts in providing flexible scheduling, childcare facilities, and other support services, although most companies have not developed an overall workable policy for dealing with the conflicting demands on employees' time.

AT THE COALFACE . . .

The controversial WorkChoices policy of the former Howard government in Australia acknowledges growing social concern about work–family balance. The Howard government published a fact sheet entitled: "Why family-friendly policies are good for business" and included several recommendations for introducing family-friendly work practices. Some of the ideas outlined included negotiating flexible start and finish times, broadening the definition of "family," allowing staff to use work mobiles for emergency family reasons, discouraging weekend work and staying back late in the office except in exceptional circumstances, and allowing leave without pay for cultural purposes.

The subsequent Rudd and Gillard governments took a step further in an effort to improve work–life balance for employees.[4]

---

[4] Wood, J. et al. (2013) *Organisational Behaviour: Core Concepts and Applications,* 3rd Australasian edition. Milton: John Wiley & Sons.

Future-thinking organizations are more and more likely to develop comprehensive programs to assist employees to manage work–home conflicts, rather than cobble together piecemeal approaches. The current realities of a market-driven workforce and the imperative to attract and keep top performers are drivers to develop flexible work arrangements that help people manage their increasingly busy lives.

What are the advantages for employers and employees?

Employees are more mobile than ever before in history: they change jobs more frequently, organizational loyalty is a thing of the past, and people are taking charge of their careers like never before. So it is worth asking the question: Why bother promoting organizational commitment? Aren't we swimming against the tide? Despite the realities of increasing worker mobility, a committed workforce has many advantages for individuals and organizations. From the perspective of the organization, It saves the firm money in the form of lower recruiting costs, fewer stranded clients, and less downtime. Organizations ought to be motivated to foster commitment from their employees as a way of achieving some stability and reducing the costs of employment turnover. Moreover, committed employees will also work harder and be more likely to "go the extra mile" to achieve organizational objectives. Organizational leaders can't stop the trend towards greater employee mobility. But they can slow down the migration rates in their own organizations and, at the same time, gain the undoubted benefits of a committed workforce.

Individual employees benefit too from an organization that actively promotes that value of commitment. A committed employee is one who has power. It follows that, the more unique and organizationally relevant a person's expertise, the greater the likelihood that a staff member will be able to exert influence within that organization. The ability to exert influence is likely to be appealing to self-motivated employees. The upshot is that they are likely to stay with the organization longer than may otherwise be the case.

In summary, increased employee commitment is based on a number of employment factors. Characteristics of a committed workforce include, but are not limited to:

- sufficiency of pay, benefits, and rewards;
- family-oriented policies and actions;
- quality of the supervisory relationship;
- favorable developmental training and experiences;
- stimulating work;
- clearly-stated guidelines defining appropriate work behavior and job demands;
- participation in goal setting;
- regular feedback on performance;
- supportive communications with immediate supervisors and upper management;
- fair and impartial performance-appraisal decisions; and
- objective measures of performance.

Of course, the reverse is true: commitment will erode if these factors are violated in some way by managers. As I said, other factors are involved in creating commitment from an organizational perspective. But adhering to these factors is a good starting point.

So, the key question for employers is: What can we (as an enterprise) do to help employees become more committed to helping us achieve our organizational goals? From an employee's perspective, the answer to this question may be: "I am willing to commit to these goals if the organization is committed to helping me achieve my personal objectives." These factors and the others outlined above can become a part of an enterprise agreement between employees and employer.

How can an enterprise agreement help to build commitment?

This process of exchanging certain commitments can form the basis of an enterprise agreement (EA) between the employees and the organization. Any of the factors I listed above are open for negotiation between employees and their employer at the enterprise level. A worthwhile EA should address some or all of the issues listed above. If the EA is perceived fairly by both the individual and organization, it is likely to increase commitment from both parties in the employment relationship. The employee commits to helping the organization achieve its output goals, and, in return, receives certain benefits.

There are widely differing systems of enterprise bargaining throughout the industrialized world. However, despite these differences there is a general trend towards the decentralization of bargaining; that is, bargaining and agreement at the organizational level. Decentralized bargaining within the organization is a more flexible and adaptable approach than an industry or nationwide approach. An EA is—in most circumstances—negotiated between both an employer and trade union acting on behalf of employees, or an employer and employees negotiating directly.

A fair and well-structured EA can benefit both employers and employees. From the employer's point of view, they act as the cornerstone of a committed workforce to achieve organizational outcomes. An EA, from an employee's perspective, can promote greater flexibility in working conditions that suit them to achieve their personal objectives. Done properly, these kinds of agreements can encourage greater commitment.

At any rate, the best way for managers to promote the value of commitment in their companies is to help employees achieve their personal objectives. As I have pointed out, proof of this commitment includes an obligation to provide employees with skills development opportunities; to put in place financial and social inducements to stay; and to invest company resources in developing people. The proper reciprocal employee response is to commit to assisting the organization to achieve its organizational outcomes. This is done by acquiring the skills provided by the company; understanding that leaving may in some way be costly to the company; and displaying a sense of obligation to the company. These mindsets are likely to lead to a value of commitment to replace the old value of loyalty.

The **10** Key Points …

1. Managers who can practically demonstrate a sense of commitment to assisting employees achieve their personal goals will—in most cases—receive commitment from their employees to achieve organizational performance goals.

2. Human spirit and work stresses the relationship between the individual and his/her work and its associated conditions. The value of commitment is concerned with the link between the individual and the organization.

3. There are three dimensions to commitment: affective commitment (desire); continuance commitment (cost); and normative commitment (obligation).

4. Affective commitment is defined as the employee's emotional attachment to the organization.

5. Continuance commitment is defined as the employee's attachment to the organization because of the perceived costs of leaving to work somewhere else.

6. Normative commitment is defined as the employee's attachment to the organization, due to obligation.

7. The following strategies can increase commitment: aligning career growth with company goals; designing work with

variety and autonomy; focusing on relationships; matching individual and organizational values; and improving work–life balance.

 There are advantages for both employees and employers in promoting organizational commitment. For organizations that foster commitment, it achieves some stability and reduces the costs of employment turnover. For employees, their commitment gives them influence.

This process of exchanging certain commitments can form the basis of an enterprise agreement (EA) between the employees and the organization.

The right response by managers in promoting the value of commitment in their companies is to help employees achieve their personal objectives. The proper reciprocal employee response is to commit to assisting the organization to achieve its organizational outcomes.

11

Three-dimensional Learning

From training to learning and development

> *A company's perspective on HRD can explain its beliefs about human nature.*

Marcia has a dilemma. One of her five work teams is performing below her expectations. She considers the array of options open to her for how to improve the team's performance. Was the problem a lack of technical skills? she wonders. On the other hand, could the problem be a nontechnical one? Could it be about the people rather than their technical competence? In terms of a solution, could the poor work performance be resolved through personal development? Yet again, perhaps it may be due to an inability to resolve the day-to-day problems that bombard the team in their work servicing a range of complex problems from an array of stakeholders across the company. Marcia decided to apply three strategic approaches to assist the underperforming team to develop and grow.

In her mind, the first step was to investigate the matter further before tackling the problem.

If the problem was related to a lack of technical skills and knowhow, Marcia thought that implementing a pay-for-performance system with the support of organizationally-sponsored skill-based training might work. This approach would, hopefully, encourage improved performance in the team through the development of the technical skills of all six team members.

A second approach Marcia had in mind was to develop the nontechnical capabilities of her team members. This approach would be based on personal development. Using this strategy, she considered recognizing publicly the top performers in the team. Marcia thought that perhaps she could post the names of people who had achieved a high standard of work on the luncheon bulletin board and implement a monthly reward ceremony. The rewards would be based on people's efficiency. In this way, she would approach the problem from the perspective of instilling pride in individual performance. Marcia thought that before this could be implemented she would have to provide her employees with some training in goal setting and time management. This approach would promote personal development of the individuals within the team.

Marcia's third option was to take a problem-solving approach to improving the team's decision-making skills. A management strategy could be used to investigate the causes of poor performance, including problem solving and brainstorming meetings with, and between, workers in that particular team. The complex nature of some of the problems affecting the team meant they often chose the wrong option. This alternative would adopt a "lateral thinking" approach to solve the myriad of problems facing the team in their everyday dealings with other functions within the company.

One—or a combination—of these three approaches may work, Marcia thought. She felt confident that the issue could now be resolved. Marcia came to the conclusion that, using a multidimensional approach, she would be more likely to be successful in resolving the challenging human resource development issues.

Now, more than ever, an organization's strategic approach to learning and development needs to be broader than simply the narrow confines of technical training. Technical training has been the conventional approach to learning and development since the birth of industry. Technical training helps employees to develop skills that enable them to do their job more capably. Although still important, modern companies and employees need more than technical skills and knowhow to survive and prosper in the twenty-first century.

Employees across all industries are facing—on a daily basis—problems, challenges, and dilemmas that can't necessarily be solved using procedural knowledge and skills. There is not always a clearly defined process to resolve some of these, increasingly complex, problems. The answers are not always found in the company manual.

Some of these dilemmas require employees to think on their feet. Traditional training does not teach people to think laterally. In fact, the opposite is the case: Training is designed to teach people processes and systems that should be followed in common situations and circumstances.

The value of learning and development is a broader interpretation of HRD than training. Training is predominantly about developing employees' technical skills and capabilities. Building technical capability is no doubt useful to employees in helping them carry out their job responsibilities and in helping them with their career path. It is also in the best interests of a business to have technically proficient employees. But the concept of learning and developing covers other dimensions of HRD.

Progressive managers—like Marcia in the vignette—take an eclectic view of HRD that includes technical and nontechnical elements of learning and development. In practice, this means investing in both technical and nontechnical HRD. Apart from potentially being more effective, managers should invest in the whole person, not just in their functional capacities. Through an emphasis on both technical and nontechnical elements, employers and employees have a greater likelihood of resolving issues in their workplace. They have more strings to their bow. This multidimensional orientation moves the organization beyond a value of training to a value of learning and development. Although all eight values in the model embrace components of HRD, the value of learning and development is primarily about a company's philosophical approach to HRD.

How is the value of training different to the value of learning and development?

The fundamental difference is that the value of learning and development takes a multi-dimensional approach to HRD. Training, on the other hand, is one-dimensional and based essentially on the production-centered approach. The person-centered and problem-solving approaches are missing from traditional HRD programs. The traditional employment relationship performance orientation is based almost exclusively on directly developing the technical job skills of employees. Yet the unpredictability associated with the contemporary marketplace and the increasing focus on the customer has elevated the importance of being able to solve unique problems and display initiative. To be flexible and enterprising is now a core capability of the modern employee. Apart from displaying appropriate initiative, the dimension of personal development and its impact on overall workplace performance is now more widely understood and accepted. Today's workplace needs a more wide-ranging approach to HRD beyond the reliance on technical training.

How is the value of learning and development defined?

There are elements related to HRD in all eight values of the model. The value of learning and development cuts across the values of flexible deployment, customer focus, performance focus, project-based work, human spirit and work, commitment, and open information. Discussions on the other seven values are primarily concerned with operation-related learning and development interventions. However, the overall philosophical dimension of HRD is an important consideration for a company. This chapter is about the overarching strategic perspective of people development. In other words, this chapter explores the overriding assumptions of HRD in an organizational context. A company's perspective on HRD can explain its beliefs about human nature.

As I mentioned earlier, there are three predominant philosophical approaches to HRD:

- the production-centered approach;
- the person-centered approach; and
- the problem-solving approach.

Each approach has a particular orientation and certain advantages and disadvantages.

Let's take a closer look at each of these HRD approaches.

Production-centered approach

The traditional method commonly adopted by most managers is the production-centered approach. A production-centered approach emphasizes the performance perspective for learning and development programs. The rationale for this approach stresses a direct link between training that focuses on enhancing current job skills and organizational performance. Consequently, the primary motive for an organization adopting this approach is to develop employees' current job skills to directly improve overall production and productivity. Of the three approaches to HRD, the production-centered approach is the one most directly related to the specifics of an employee's job performance.

For example, training programs that improve employees' mastery of the use of machines, technology, or processes that are connected directly to the job an employee does are production-centered.

Production-centered learning is likely to have a direct payoff in terms of increasing the productivity of employees. The measure of success of training—based on the production-centered approach— is whether or not the learning experience translates into a more technically proficient employee.

From an employee's point of view, the primary incentive for undertaking production-centered training is greater technical mastery of their current job, to help them complete their organizational tasks with greater skill. This approach and its attraction to both managers and employees has been embraced and argued for passionately by many authors, particularly those who advocate competency-based training.

The fundamental weakness of the production-centered approach is that it favors the interests of the organization before considering the interests of the employee. A purely production-centered approach is based on the notion that individuals play a role in organizations and can therefore be viewed as abstract and anonymous job-holders or performers. The overriding assumption is that employees passively react to stimuli in the organizational environment. It is true that the employee can also gain career-enhancing skills from the production-centered approach. However, these job skills are based first and foremost on the needs and priorities of the organization. The needs of the individual worker are a secondary consideration.

Person-centered approach

A second philosophical perspective on learning and HRD is the person-centered approach. This approach emphasizes personal development. Person-centered learning stresses an indirect link between the learning experience and work performance.

The primary motive for an organizational leader to invest in personal development learning is to enhance employees' personal qualities that will have a positive impact on their overall work performance.

Unlike the production-centered approach, the person-centered approach has a more tenuous link to performance. It is based on the theory that capable people make capable employees in a variety of contexts.

For example, training programs that improve people's mastery of themselves—such as courses on goal setting, personal motivation, time management, and emotional intelligence—can have a resultant payoff in terms of increased productivity. The incentive to sponsor personal development programs for the organization is based on the premise that by developing the most precious organizational resource—people—the company is likely to stimulate them to be more proficient in their current and future work practices. Over the last quarter of a century, the growing popularity of this HRD approach would suggest that this argument is well founded.

From the employees' perspective, the motivation to undertake person-centered learning is the opportunity to develop themselves and therefore improve and enrich their career prospects. In other words, the attraction is broadening the scope of their skill sets beyond their technical competence. Of the two approaches, the person-centered approach has traditionally been less appealing to organizational leaders because of the weaker connection between the learning experience and current job outputs.

AT THE COALFACE . . .

The Sir Edmund Hillary Outdoor Pursuits Centre of New Zealand was founded in 1972. The late Sir Edmund Hillary was a patron of the Centre. The vision of the center is to provide people with the opportunity to take part in adventurous outdoor activities. People who take part in such adrenalin-producing activities tend to experience intrinsic changes. Positive gains are made in self-esteem, skills are developed, and social interactions are enhanced. Competition is subdued while cooperation is encouraged. A number of successful corporations have put staff and managers through outdoor programs such as those offered by the center. Through these experiences, participants explore values and recognize weaknesses in themselves, and have the potential to create positive changes in themselves and their organizations.[1]

---

[1] Outdoor Pursuits Centre (2008) History of OPC. At www.opc.org.nz, accessed January 2014.

Regardless of the rhetoric of the person-centered approach, in reality this strategy can also subordinate the individual to organizational needs and interests. For example, employees attending a personal development training program are often placed in a position where they are required to follow organizationally-sponsored trainers and set program content. Trainees may be given little option but to simply follow what the trainer says. There is most likely no requirement for participants to engage in independent thinking. The trained person simply acts on the basis of direction from the trainer or on the contents of a training manual. These personal development courses, like the vast majority of technical training, are often "how to" or procedurally driven.

For instance, a program on communication might stress the five steps to improving listening skills and explain that process in detail for participants to implement. Undoubtedly, procedural knowledge gained this way is valuable and necessary for some tasks. However, too much attention on procedural knowledge training has the potential to undercut the capacity for real personal development. So, in certain circumstances, the person-centered approach can undermine an individual's fundamental and inherent self-determination.

Both the product- and person-centered approaches to learning and development are valuable and have their place in organization and people development. But they can reinforce the idea that the needs of the organization are more important than the needs of the employee.

Problem-solving approach

The third school of HRD thinking is referred to as the problem-solving approach. The focus of this approach is on improving employees' ability to solve problems. This approach improves employees' ability to make more effective decisions on the job. The rationale for this approach is the direct and indirect connection between problem-solving capability and organizational performance. In other words, the primary motive for organizational leaders to invest in problem-solving learning is to improve employees' decision-making aptitude, so they can better deal with unpredictable challenges in their job.

This HRD approach is based on the theory that individuals are likely to make better decisions in their everyday work if they have the necessary knowledge, skills, and mindsets to analyze random problems. Consequently, employees are likely to exercise greater autonomy in dealing with ambiguous issues affecting their work. This is likely to result is less dependence on their supervisor.

For example, topics such as creative problem-solving techniques, research skills, or analysis of typical workplace case studies can develop problem-solving capabilities.

Most managers' motives for using the problem-solving approach are based on the belief that developing employees' problem-solving abilities is likely to stimulate faster and better-quality decision-making throughout the organization. Quicker and improved execution of daily challenges is likely to result in better customer service. Apart from this attraction for managers, greater employee self-sufficiency is likely to place less strain on managerial resources.

Employees' motivation to learn problem-solving skills is likely to be so that they are less reliant on their boss to make decisions affecting their daily work. Employees therefore have more freedom and confidence to make decisions. Furthermore, employees can be attracted to problem-solving learning opportunities in order to improve their overall employability. It is not surprising, therefore, that this HRD approach is gaining more prominence in an increasingly complex and less predictable working environment.

The problem-solving approach should be jointly considered with the person- and production-centered perspectives. Today, the ability to think laterally, creatively, and flexibly is critical to success in any field of work. The pressure of global competition means that each customer's needs must be treated individually and standard problem-solving approaches are not always going to work, or be appropriate. Being able to take an exceptional situation and deal with it efficiently and effectively is a skill that is important to the customer, employee, and company.

AT THE COALFACE . . .

Julie—Executive Manager of Learning and Development for a large, well-known bank—was charged with responsibility for revamping the bank's approach to inducting customer service representatives (CSRs) in retail banking services. After looking at the turnover rates and gathering information from a series of interviews with staff, she decided it was time to act.

From what she had heard in these conversations, the bank had a challenge to reduce the high rates of turnover in CSRs in the first twelve weeks of their employment. Employees had told their managers in these conversations that they lacked confidence in their skills and knowledge. The approach in the induction program was the place to start, she concluded.

From a learning perspective, the new approach enabled participants to better analyze situations and source information more effectively. This policy, supported by a continuous coaching component, involved a partnership between the participant, their branch manager, and a "buddy" who was an experienced CSR. With this support, participants were required to take ownership of their learning and complete a series of tasks. In addition to this, they would work with their branch manager to identify strengths and areas of improvement through daily check-ins, debriefs, and feedback sessions.

Collaborative learning occurs through the use of problem-based learning, simulations, and research. During off-the-job learning periods, participants would work in learning sets or groups to explore customer situations they would encounter in real life. They were encouraged to analyze the situation, explore how they would respond to it, and complete any customer transactions using simulations or role play.

To date, the CSR induction program was able to deliver an 8 percent reduction in voluntary turnover in the first six months.[2]

---

[2] Baker, T.B. (2013) *The End of the Performance Review: A New Approach to Appraising Employee Performance*. London: Palgrave Macmillan.

What are the elements of learning and development?

Similar to the other seven values in the New Employment Relationship Model, applying the value of learning and development is a joint responsibility between employer and employee. From the perspective of the organization, the three key elements are the provision of a balanced HRD program that includes job, problem solving, and personal development HRD opportunities for employees. From the individual perspective, the corresponding key elements are a willingness to participate in these three types of learning opportunities. These provisions, and the willingness to participate in a multidimensional approach to HRD, is likely to shift the value from one of training to a broader value of learning and development.

What is the multidimensional approach?

Notwithstanding the fact that there are strong advocates and arguments for each of these three approaches, undoubtedly the most effective way of aligning the needs and interests of individual and organization is by using an eclectic approach. A multidimensional strategy is a more comprehensive approach to learning and development that brings to light the strengths of each HRD perspective. It is not really a question of which philosophical approach is the best. A far more constructive question for organizational leaders is: What does each approach have to offer in terms of dealing with workplace issues?

Understanding the basis of each approach can make managers more informed about their choices in HRD. For example, a team leader who is faced with the challenge of improving lagging work performance with his/her team might deal with this issue in three different ways. From the person-centered perspective, the issue could be tackled from a personal efficiency point of view. (That is, the issue could be one of improving the way the team manages their workload and time.) This may take the form of implementing a training program in time management. By doing so, the team leader is tackling the issue from a person-centered perspective. From another perspective, the manager may consider the issue from the point of view of low technical competence. The team leader may tackle this with a production-centered approach. For instance, employees may then undertake a competency-based training program, such as courses in administrative and clerical skill development. Yet a third option open to the team leader is to take a problem-solving approach. Using this approach, the team leader may facilitate a workshop to improve communication with other departments within the company. The workshop could discuss some of the key issues affecting the team's performance and how to improve communication links with one or more functional areas. Any one of these, or a combination of these, approaches may help to improve performance.

Organizational leaders who can select from a number of different perspectives to solve HRD challenges have a wider array of possible solutions than one who only applies one philosophical approach to solving learning and development issues. It therefore stands to reason that the organizational leader using the multidimensional approach is more likely to be successful at resolving challenging HRD issues.

In terms of managing this HRD multidimensional approach, I would suggest that approximately one-third of an organization's budget should be devoted to each approach. One-third of the budget could be committed to the self-development of employees (person-centered approach), one-third to specific training to carry out organization roles with greater skill and competence (production-centered approach), and one-third to developing problem-solving capabilities (problem-solving approach). This mix of learning and development approaches can reinforce the legitimacy of HRD, contribute significantly to balancing the learning and development needs of individuals and the organization, and provide managers with a broader learning and development framework for solving organizational issues.

In the New Employment Relationship Model (outlined in Chapter 4), the individual corresponding accountability for the value of learning and development is to be committed to lifelong learning. This mindset is present when there is a willingness to learn job skills, problem-solving skills, and personal development skills. From the organizational perspective, the corresponding accountability is to enter into a partnership for employee development. This is likely to be accomplished with the organization's commitment to provide job, problem solving, and personal development learning opportunities. These elements and the matching individual and organizational responses are likely to modify the culture of the organization from a value of training to a value of learning and development.

The **10** Key Points …

1. Now, more than ever, an organization's strategic approach to learning and development needs to be broader than simply the narrow confines of technical training.

2. The fundamental difference is that the value of learning and development takes a multidimensional approach to HRD. Training, on the other hand, is one-dimensional and based on the production-centered approach.

3. There are three predominant philosophical approaches to HRD. These three approaches are the production-centered approach, person-centered approach, and problem-solving approach.

4. The primary motive for an organization adopting the production-centered approach is to develop employees' current job skills to directly improve overall productivity.

5. The primary motive for an organizational leader to invest in the person-centered approach is to enhance employees' personal qualities which will ultimately have a positive impact on their overall work performance.

6. The primary motive for organizational leaders to invest in the problem-centered approach is to improve employees' decision-making ability, so they can deal with unpredictable challenges in their job.

7 From the perspective of the organization, the three key elements are the provision of a balanced HRD program that includes job, problem solving, and personal development HRD opportunities for employees.

8 From the individual perspective, the corresponding key elements are a willingness to participate in these three types of learning opportunities.

9 The most effective approach in terms of aligning the needs and interests of individual and organization is an eclectic approach. A multidimensional strategy is a comprehensive approach to learning and development that brings to light the strengths of each HRD perspective.

10 One-third of the budget should be committed to the self-development of employees (person-centered approach), one-third to specific training to carry out organization roles with greater skill and competence (production-centered approach), and one-third to developing problem-solving capabilities (problem-solving approach).

12

Overcoming the Initiative Paradox

From closed information to open information

> How can managers constrain employees' independent judgment and, at the same, encourage initiative?

Rachel received a phone call from an irate customer. The conversation went like this: "Your last invoice overcharged me on my telephone account by $149.90. I'm not happy about it and want it fixed straight away," said Charlie Robertson, the fuming customer.

"OK, Mr. Robertson, let me bring up your account details on my screen," replied a nervous Rachel.

"Yes, there appears to be a mistake, Mr. Robertson, according to our records. I will need to talk to my manager about this and get back to you," Rachel went on.

"Why do you need to talk to your boss if it is obvious that you have made a mistake in your billing?" asked the customer, in a threatening tone.

"That's company policy, Mr. Robertson," replied Rachel.

Rachel immediately went to speak with Margaret, her manager, about Mr. Robertson's situation. Margaret looked at Rachel and said, after studying *the paperwork, "Obviously, there is an error. Call the customer back immediately and let him know that we'll amend this mistake in our next invoice."*

Just as Rachel was about to leave Margaret's office, Margaret said, "OK, let's set a rule here, Rachel. From now on, if a customer calls and complains, and it's obvious that we have made an error and it involves a sum of $200 or less, then I want you to fix it straight away without consulting me. That way, we are unlikely to antagonize the customer any more than is necessary. I want you to show initiative in future under these circumstances, OK?"

Rachel called the customer back to reassure him. Mr. Robertson responded with, "Thank you, but I don't understand why you needed to talk to your manager if the situation was obviously a mistake."

Rachel now understood why Margaret wanted her to show initiative if the billing error in future was less than $200.

So far, in this book I have suggested that employers need employees who are flexible, customer- and performance-focused, project-based, engaged, committed, and open to growing and developing. Similarly, employees require employers to give them the opportunity to work in a variety of settings, provide them with information, skills, and incentives to focus on the customer, reward them for good performance, involve them in projects, give them meaningful work, commit to helping them to achieve their personal goals, and enter into a partnership for their growth and development. This is the basis for the New Employment Relationship Model.

To achieve all this, employees need access to information: they need channels of open information. Organizations should provide employees with access to information about organizational goals, needs, and human resource systems. Employers ought to be prepared to share information with their employees to enable them to be more enterprising. In exchange, employees should be willing to contribute to the organizational decision-making processes by showing appropriate initiative.

In other words, the value now is about opening information channels rather than closing off information. The traditional employment relationship was characterized by managers being selective about what information they shared with their employees. "You will be told on a need-to-know basis" was a common phase. Employees consequently responded by being compliant and doing what they were told, rather than displaying initiative. Employees were unable or unwilling to display initiative because they didn't have the same perspective as their managers. The value of open information encourages employees to display initiative because their perspective ought to be similar to that of their manager.

Why is open information so important now?

The shared value of open information is an important part of the New Employment Relationship Model for several good reasons. Like the other values in the model, it cuts across other values. However, opening communication channels is so important that it has become an explicit value of the model. The importance of open communication; the commercial advantages; the relevance of participation in decision making; and the fact that employees want a greater degree of autonomy are reasons for its inclusion. These are briefly outlined below.

References in literature

Most books and articles written about change management and organizational culture generally point out the importance and relevance of improving the flow of information within and beyond an organization. For instance, authors talk about the value and relevance of clear communication between managers and their staff. The value of communication between an organization and its customer base has already been discussed in Chapter 6. One of the reasons for including the value of open information is how often it is mentioned as an important feature of a healthy organization.

Commercial advantages

There is no doubt that many benefits stem from open information. As I have mentioned throughout this book, businesses profit from having a flexible, adaptable, and responsive organizational structure. These characteristics are likely to come from a culture that is willing to share information across and down the business. It is this sharing and communicating of important information that assists employees to make better-quality decisions each and every day.

Participative values

As I have also mentioned in this book, there has been renewed interest in participative values, cultures, and everyday practices of organizations as they operate in an increasingly competitive global market. It therefore follows that a more participative approach can only be achieved through open communication between employer and employee.

Autonomy

Closely associated with participative values is evidence supporting the notion that the majority of enlightened employees want to have more autonomy and show more initiative and participation in organizational decision-making processes. To be more involved in their work, employees need a flow of quality information from their managers to inform them when and where they can display their initiative.

These four factors legitimize the value of open information in the New Employment Relationship Model, and form an important base for becoming an employer of choice.

Southwest Airlines empowers its managers and front-line staff—those who deal daily with customers—to act as "problem solvers," often making decisions on the spot that can save a relationship with a customer. In the airline industry, a company is only as good as its customers' last travel experience. Ginger Hardage, Southwest's senior vice president for corporate communication, recently told participants at a conference a story about a Southwest pilot:

On September 11, 2001, after terrorists had brought the Twin Towers down, all other planes that were already in the air were grounded. A Southwest plane was directed to land at an airport that Southwest did not serve, and the passengers and crew were put up in a hotel. When Southwest management called the hotel to inquire about the passengers and crew, they were told that no one was there—the pilot had taken everyone who had been on that plane out to the movies.

"There's no manual from which to learn that," said Hardage. "At Southwest, employees are encouraged to make decisions from the heart, and in turn, these proactive gestures provide positive benefits to the customers and the company."

Corporate cultures such as Southwest's take commitment from the boardroom down to front-line employees. They're not "programs" or "tactics," but a way of life.

Hardage, who heads Southwest Airlines' internal and external communication, shared some thoughts about the role of communications in fostering a positive corporate culture.

Companies must provide the level of knowledge and information that allows employees to "act like owners." Southwest Airlines provides daily news updates via its intranet; the CEO records a weekly telephone message for all employees; and the company communicates detailed financial information called "Knowing the Score" on quarterly earnings. More than 14 percent of outstanding shares of stock are held by Southwest employees.

Southwest communicates with employees every day through news on their intranet, every week through a telephone news line, every month with a 32-page magazine, and every quarter through the financial "Knowing the Score" message, and every year through a series of town hall meetings.

Communicators must nurture their corporate cultures so that employees understand how their behavior contributes to how their organizations are judged. In its monthly newsletter *LUVLines*, Southwest features employees who have been nominated by their peers for "Winning Spirit" recognition. These outstanding employees are modeling the type of proactive behavior that results in a remarkable, instead of an ordinary, experience for a customer or fellow employee.[1]

---

[1] "Southwest's Secret to a Positive Corporate Culture: Its Employees." At http://mere6245.wordpress.com/2008/07/05/corporate-culture/, accessed January 2014.

Why is it such a challenge to get employees to show initiative?

The initiative paradox[2] is defined as managing the extent and limits of employee participation in decision making. It is therefore tied

---

[2] The term "initiative paradox" comes from Campbell, D.J. (2000) "The proactive employee: Managing workplace initiative." *Academy of Management Executive* 14(3), 52–66.

to the flow and quality of information that provides a responsive environment to enable appropriate participation by employees in organizational decision making. I mentioned in Chapter 2 that the drive to empower employees is becoming stronger. As a consequence, the challenge of resolving the initiative paradox involves greater numbers of employees and their managers across more and more industry groups. If modern companies are to flourish in this volatile global environment and meet challenges such as geographical dispersion, electronic collaboration, and cultural diversity, they need to encourage open information systems.

From the perspective of the employee, opening up communication systems promises to equip them to become more knowledgeable, self-sufficient, participative, adaptive, flexible, efficient, and responsive to rapid change. The value of having employees participate in implementing projects and programs has universal application. Managing employee initiative is therefore an ongoing concern for all organizations and has benefits for employees too. Nonetheless, there are still plenty of examples of inconsistencies in terms of managing the initiative paradox across a range of organizational settings.

How can you get people in the workplace to show initiative when they need to? And at the same time, how do you get them to follow company guidelines and processes when they have to? Managers have tried to implement company rules, regulations, policies, and guidelines as a way of resolving the initiative paradox. Some strategies have been successful, but many have failed.

I am sure you can think of daily examples of when you see too much initiative—or not enough.

Consider, for example, a retail franchise business.

Staff will often talk about ownership when they refer to their involvement in retail outlets. They are probably multi-skilled in all the tasks involved in running a retail store. These same employees will often question what they perceive to be unnecessary interference by head office in the running of "their" store. This may include such things as policy making, customer interaction, purchasing, stock control, and systems and procedures. This often creates tension between head office and individual franchises. Employees see that their initiative to make decisions at the "coalface" is being sabotaged by head office. This results from employees' perception that managers will interfere in their areas of influence, so they become less inclined to display initiative. So, this lack of resourcefulness by staff is viewed by management as a sign that employees in the stores cannot, or will not, take the initiative when needed. Head office becomes frustrated with front-line employees whom they perceive to be relying too heavily on them to make decisions that they consider to be daily operational matters. Management from head office therefore feels reluctantly justified to make decisions in operational matters. This "vicious cycle" leads to frustration on the parts of both employees and managers.

How do we overcome the initiative paradox?

According to David Campbell, there are four practical strategies to help overcome the initiative paradox. These are:

- goal alignment;
- boundary refinement;
- information sharing; and
- active accountability.[3]

Let's look at each of these in no particular order.

---

[3] Campbell, D.J. (2000) "The proactive employee: Managing workplace initiative." *Academy of Management Executive* 14(3), 52–66.

Goal alignment

Goal alignment is about aligning the perspectives of staff and management. Where there is agreement between the motives of employer and employee, it is less likely that, when employees exercise their own judgment, it will not be in conflict with their manager. On the other hand, where there is nonalignment between both entities, employee initiative is not likely to be welcomed by management. The assumption reinforcing the goal alignment approach is that conflict is not the result of the enterprising qualities of employees; rather, it is the result of a misalignment between the organization and the individual.

Misalignment between individuals and an organization is often the result of poorly thought-out and implemented reward systems. Inappropriate performance measures can create confusion and conflict. A typical instance of this would be a company that openly values teamwork, but actually rewards individual performance. This will—and often does—discourage proactive teamwork. For example, shop attendants in a retail outlet who receive bonuses for the sale of products or services are likely to favor individual sales activity over teamwork. So, supportive practical teamwork such as exchanging sales leads between shop attendants in that store is less likely to occur. Performance management systems can suppress initiative considered important by managers. Reward systems have the potential to encourage or discourage goal alignment.

Then again, goal alignment between employees and management can be created by implementing and communicating a reward and bonus system that promotes enterprising behavior. In the above example, if the company truly values teamwork over individual performance, it would be sensible to reward shop attendants for exchanging leads, irrespective of whether this leads to a successful sale or not. By rewarding the actions that lead to a sale, rather than the sale itself, teamwork is encouraged. Doing so will foster goal alignment.

Aside from formal recognition, managers can informally foster or discourage goal alignment. A manager can send mixed signals during casual discussions with staff. For example, a manager may insist on being kept informed about all interactions with customers, on the one hand, and expect staff to show initiative on the other. When informed about an approach made by an employee to a customer, the manager may chastise the employee for their particular approach. This may inadvertently create confusion in the mind of the staff member. If the manager criticizes the staff member for the approach, without praising them for showing initiative, the staff member may interpret this as criticism for showing initiative. The outcome is goal misalignment, the opposite of what may be desired by the manager.

Some practical measures organizational leaders can take to align the goals of employees and employers are:

• Putting in place a clearly-defined formal performance bonus system.
• Managers setting an example or "walking the talk."
• Consistent informal communication between managers and their staff.
• Performance appraisals that focus on aligning individual and organization goals.

Boundary refinement

Boundary refinement is a second way of overcoming the initiative paradox. This involves a manager carefully communicating the kind of initiative s/he wants and doesn't want. In other words, this is about communicating the extent and limits of an individual's authority to display workplace initiative. Explaining when, where, and how initiative is expected spells out to employees the limits of using their initiative. If these boundaries are not communicated, employees will be confused and indecisive about displaying their initiative in the business. The assumption underpinning this strategy is that in certain situations it is appropriate and expected that employees demonstrate initiative but in other situations it is inappropriate to show initiative.

Like goal alignment, given the complexities of organizational environments, this strategy is often easier to suggest than to accomplish. Nonetheless, when employees are confused about the extent and limits of displaying initiative, it is usually because managers have not clarified and communicated these boundaries.

Furthermore, these boundaries are often not static. They can change over time and with different situations. The essence of good management in these circumstances is to be aware of these potentially changing situations and circumstances, and to quickly communicate expectations to staff when there are variations. Apart from communicating these boundaries on a regular basis, managers should use a mixture of approaches to explain the boundaries of appropriate enterprising behavior. These communication strategies may include staff meetings and discussions, coaching individuals, inducting new staff, using critical incidents and cases as examples to clarify their expectations, and written instructions.

To illustrate my point, consider a common and unanticipated dilemma facing an airline. In a circumstance where an airplane has been grounded due to unforeseen mechanical difficulties, what are the roles and responsibilities of all staff? To clarify and communicate boundaries with staff in this situation, a workshop could be organized by management. Participants may consist of a functional cross-section of the company, including pilots, flight attendants, engineers, customer service representatives, salespeople, and operational crew. In discussing this scenario, the focus would be on the various functional areas and how they would communicate and minimize inconvenience to customers on board, and get the plane in the air as soon as possible. This case study approach encouraged participants to clarify when, where, and how each function could—and should—show initiative in resolving this common problem.

Since the approach of boundary refinement works by limiting employees' initiative to highly defined and clear circumstances and situations, this strategy is especially attractive to managers who feel uncomfortable relying too heavily on the independent judgment of employees. On the other hand, this approach may hold little appeal in situations where managers wish to use employees' initiative more broadly.

Some practical measures that can be taken by managers to communicate boundaries around displaying proper initiatives are:

- Using critical incidents in the business to illustrate and clarify boundaries around using initiative.
- Coaching and mentoring employees in their work.
- Documenting acceptable and unacceptable forms of initiative.
- Rewarding appropriate initiative.

Information sharing

Information sharing between employee and employer can build trust. This approach concentrates on minimizing unshared expectations by providing employees with the same information, perspective, and frame of reference that management uses in managing their area of responsibility. The underlying assumption of this approach is that by sharing information, and therefore showing trust, employees and managers will have a similar perspective on a range of important business matters.

This method encourages employees to show initiative from an appropriate flow of information from organizational leaders. Information sharing is a particularly useful approach in the areas of strategic planning and continuous improvement. To illustrate the practical use of this strategy, a manager, using the services of a professional and independent facilitator, organizes a staff retreat as a means of promoting the exchange of important information. The purpose of the retreat is to facilitate the process of developing a five-year plan for the department, involving all staff. The manager may begin by sharing his/her vision, mission, and values with the team and invite them to work together to develop a structured five-year plan. The facilitator works with departmental staff to develop several goals that cover the manager's vision. As an extension of these goals the team works on creating a series of strategies, plans of action, accountabilities, and timelines to meet these goals. This exercise encourages employees to be involved in, and initiate, a strategic plan. From this retreat it is likely that this information-sharing exercise will result in employees and managers "being on the same page." This common understanding is likely to instill confidence in employees to display initiative when the need arises.

Another practical, simple, and effective information-sharing exercise involves continuous improvement. A group of employees are invited to document an issue that they believe needs improvement within the area of their control. With several issues raised, the team are then invited to vote on the issue they believe to be the most pressing or relevant. The top issues are prioritized and employees are invited to work in project teams to develop improvement strategies using a structured approach. These plans are then documented. For this process to be workable, managers provide useful information that helps the project teams to develop practical improvements. By exchanging information, the end result in the process of developing a continuous improvement plan is likely to be an alignment of perspectives between all participants.

In these two information-sharing exercises, the manager essentially shares the managerial role with the staff. Employees gain an understanding of their manager's perspective on important issues, procedures, and policies. This alignment of thinking comes from the manager freely sharing and exchanging work unit information and strategies with staff. Such openness and sharing can mean that the manager is to some extent exposed and more dependent on staff. The information-sharing strategy can bring about higher levels of trust between the organizational leaders and members.

Some key steps you can take to share information include:

- Holding annual strategic planning days.
- Running continuous improvement workshops.
- Group problem-solving sessions.
- Regular staff meetings.

Active accountability

Active accountability involves an understanding between managers and staff that initiative and judgment can be exercised, but only at the particular employee's own risk. In other words, if the result of employee initiative is unacceptable to management, it can adversely affect the initiator. This kind of strategy is typically commonplace in bureaucratic and authority-focused organizations, such as the military. These kinds of organizations rely on a clearly-defined chain of command for decision making. The underlying assumption here is that there is recognition that at times you can and should display initiative. But the initiator should always be ultimately accountable for his/her proactive behavior.

For example, consider an employee in charge of purchasing stock in a large corporation with very stringent purchasing rules and regulations. One of those policies may be to order in products at a specified time of the month. But the employee may have advance notice that the company has won a large contract with a customer. This customer requires immediate delivery of the product. Under these circumstances, the person in charge decides to order outside the normal ordering cycle to respond to the immediate needs of the customer. This enterprising behavior exhibited by the employee violates a major company policy. But by showing initiative the employee delights the customer with quick responsiveness, and management does not criticize this staff member's behavior.

Consider another case in a military context where a squad leader may refuse a potentially illegal order from a direct superior. For example, a superior orders a subordinate to cover up the details of a murder before an official investigation takes place. By not doing so, the squad leader is violating a command. While the subordinate may suffer initially from insubordination from the commanding officer, he will probably not suffer negative consequences beyond the confines of the military unit. To cover these kinds of circumstances, the organization wants employees to use independent judgment, but with the associated knowledge that the organization treats errors in such judgments harshly.

AT THE COALFACE . . .

Ravi moved to Australia from India to find work to support his family back in India. He quickly found a job with a building company as a casual laborer and then became a permanent employee. Over the ten months Ravi worked for the company, the racial taunts aimed at him became more frequent, louder, and nastier. Many of his colleagues used offensive race-based names and insults in his presence and spoke to him aggressively.

Finally, Ravi had had enough and complained to the company director, who spoke to the employees to find out whether Ravi's claims were true. They admitted to making some of the comments, but said they were only jokes and not meant personally. The director told the workers that their behavior was unacceptable.

After that, Ravi's colleagues refused to speak to him at all, and refused to work with him. A week after the director's discussion with the crew, Ravi was placed back on casual status and was gradually offered less and less work and, eventually, no work at all. Ravi was at a loss to know what to do, because he and his family back home depended on the money he earned. Surfing the internet one evening to look for an answer to his dilemma, he found the Australian Human Rights Commission website and read its information.

"Maybe I should make a claim. What can I lose? Maybe I'll get my job back."

Ravi did complain. The company agreed to mediation, which failed, and then to conciliation. In the end, Ravi was paid $7,000 compensation, provided with a written reference and the company agreed to pay for anti-discrimination training for its staff.[4]

---

[4] Cole, K. (2010) *Management Theory and Practice*. Frenchs Forest: Pearson Australia, pp. 1080–81.

As you can probably imagine, active accountability is the least effective of the four approaches in promoting employee initiative. Unlike the other three strategies, active accountability does not specifically define the circumstances when initiative should take place. But at the same time, leaders using this strategy acknowledge that exceptional circumstances may call for initiative to be shown and the rules bent. Uncertainty around whether to bend the rules or not means that employees will always think twice before taking proactive action. And in these circumstances it is easier for the organization to blame employees for not following the rules if their actions cause a problem for the organization. In other words, employees cannot be certain the organization will support their judgment. Managers will evaluate proactive employee decisions dynamically, on a case-by-case basis, with hindsight knowledge of the ultimate consequences of the decision. Using this approach, the resolution of the initiative paradox has several organizational advantages, but holds few benefits for employees. It is therefore likely that employees will limit their initiative to extraordinary circumstances.

Here are some circumstances where active accountability may be considered appropriate:

• Conducting workplace investigations.
• Showing initiative against unethical behavior.
• Reporting unlawful behavior.
• Crisis management.

By using these four approaches, organizational leaders can overcome two important challenges to conquer the initiative paradox. The first challenge is to motivate individuals to use their initiative in decision making in a way that is linked with the needs of the business. The second challenge is that different situations require different forms of initiative. All four strategies attempt to limit undesirable forms of initiative. Boundary refinement and active accountability do this by limiting initiative to certain situations. Alternatively, goal alignment and information sharing encourage suitable employee initiative by creating shared perspectives with their manager. Managers should think carefully about when and where they can use each of these strategies to overcome the initiative paradox.

The four strategies I have outlined here place limits on undesirable forms of initiative and at the same time encourage initiative in appropriate ways. The common factor in using all these strategies is open communication between employees and managers. To support appropriate proactive behavior from employees, managers need to open up the communication channels. By doing this, managers give their staff the same outlook as they have. Employees also benefit: they know where and when to be more involved in decision-making situations.

What are the elements of open information?

Like the other seven values in the model, accountability for developing a value of open information rests with both the individual and organization. The four key elements for the organizational leader are to use goal alignment, boundary refinement, information sharing, and active accountability strategies wherever and whenever possible. Individuals ought to respond by showing appropriate initiative wherever and whenever possible. Evidence of this is likely to help the workplace move from a value of closed information to open information.

What are some practical open information strategies?

Well-managed firms use a combination of techniques to address the initiative paradox. For instance, managers wanting to encourage initiative put strategies in place that bring into line individual and organization goals (goal alignment). To achieve this, managers share company information with staff (information sharing). This strategy aligns individual and organizational objectives. On the other hand, companies that want to confine employees' initiative to certain activities will clarify the limits of enterprising behavior (boundary refinement) and the consequences of inappropriate initiative (active accountability). Boundary refinement and active accountability are natural pairings, and are most likely to be used together. Other strategic combinations are possible, but less likely, and specific situations or job requirements would determine those particular mixes. Poorly-managed companies characterized by low levels of enterprise by employees fail to consistently put in place these practical strategies.

Table 12.1 summarizes several workplace opportunities for each of the four strategies.

Table 12.1   Open information activities

Approach	Aim of the approach	Activities
Goal alignment	To align individual and organizational goals	• Clearly define and target formal performance bonuses • Model goal-related activity by management • Consistently communicate goals informally with staff • Appraise performance that focuses on aligning individual and organization goals • Implement succession planning
Boundary refinement	To clarify when, where and how initiative can be exercised	• Use process mapping • Use critical incidents • Coach and mentor • Document boundaries • Reward appropriate initiative
Information sharing	To share information designed to align the perspectives of management and staff	• Facilitate strategic planning workshops • Coordinate continuous improvement workshops • Run interactive meetings to solve problems • Chair regular whole-staff meetings
Active accountability	To communicate that, under certain circumstances, showing initiative is appropriate but that people, not the organization, are accountable for their actions	• Disclosure and nondisclosure of information from workplace investigations • Report unethical behavior • Report unlawful behavior • Exercise initiative in a crisis

Below, I discuss briefly each of the activities listed in Table 12.1.

Goal alignment activities

Clearly-defined formal performance bonus system

A performance bonus system that is directly linked to desirable enterprising behaviors is most likely to encourage appropriate employee initiative and so contribute to the alignment of goals between individual and organization.

Role modeling by management

If managers are not "walking the talk," then it is likely that staff will follow their pattern of behavior. For example, if the senior management team is not operating as a cohesive team, as one of the stated goals of the organization, then it is likely that other teams in the organization will not display good teamwork. The result is goal misalignment.

Consistent informal communication

The consequences of what managers say to staff in informal conversations in the hallway, bathroom, or by the water cooler are often underestimated by organizational leaders. For instance, if two managers give out inconsistent messages to the same staff member, no matter where or when, it will undoubtedly create confusion and consequently, goal misalignment.

Performance appraisals that focus on aligning individual and organization goals

A fair amount of a performance appraisal discussion ought to be devoted to matching an employee's skill set and interests to assisting the organization achieve its outcomes. But this is often not the case. This is an important element of the value of human spirit and work (see Chapter 9). (I have written a book on this topic: *The End of the Performance Review: A New Approach to Appraising Employee Performance*. London: Palgrave Macmillan.)

Succession planning

Grooming junior employees for more senior positions within the organization is an important way of matching the goals of an individual with the needs of the organization.

Boundary refinement activities

Use of process mapping

Process mapping is a potent way of identifying and obtaining agreement on where, when, and how employees can, and should, display their initiative. At the same time, it is a useful tool for pointing out when enterprising behavior is inappropriate.

Figure 12.1 shows a simple example of a process map illustrating a florist's online ordering process.

Using a visual representation of a business process, such as the example shown in Figure 12.1, can be a vehicle for pinpointing opportunities to show initiative and also parts of the process that requires employees not to be proactive.

Use of critical incidents

Using a critical incident or a real-life case can assist managers and staff to clarify suitable opportunities to exhibit initiative in comparable situations in the future.

Coaching and mentoring

All one-on-one coaching and mentoring opportunities are ideal opportunities for explaining to employees the parameters of initiative in their work.

Documenting boundaries

Documenting situations when initiative should be displayed can be outlined in the company handbook or intranet site. This can be a helpful reference for employees.

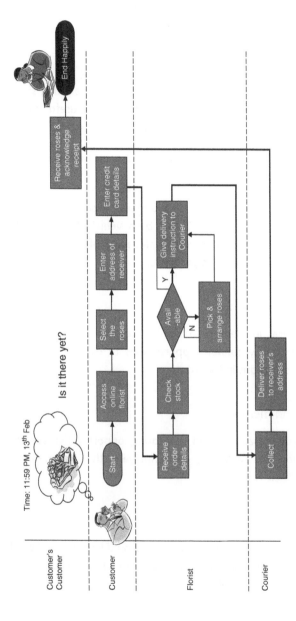

FIG 12.1 A florist's online ordering process

This figure was originally published in Baker, T.B. (2009) *The 8 Values of Highly Productive Companies: Creating Wealth From a New Employment Relationship.* Brisbane, Australian Academic Press.

Rewarding appropriate initiative

When enterprising behavior has been exhibited by an employee, an effective way to reinforce the value of this behavior is by rewarding or recognizing the person for his/her efforts.

Information-sharing activities

Strategic planning workshops

Annual retreats for all staff in a department or organization to review the year and plan for the future can be an effective way to align employer/employee perspectives.

Continuous improvement workshops

Getting an organizational department, function, or team together to review its processes and systems is potentially a highly effective way of bringing into line the views of managers and staff.

Problem-solving meetings

Problem-solving meetings with staff and management can get both parties on the same wavelength.

Regular whole-staff meetings

Whole-staff meetings once a month or once a quarter are useful forums in which to share company information with everyone.

Active accountability activities

Workplace investigations

Workplace investigations may at times require the person undertaking the investigation to show initiative when unanticipated information surfaces. For example, if s/he hears a conflicting account of how an accident occurred, he/she will be obliged to explore that account.

Showing initiative against unethical behavior

Employee's careers can sometimes be adversely affected by drawing attention to unethical workplace behavior or practices. However, in the majority of cases, showing appropriate initiative in these circumstances is deemed legitimate and reasonable.

Reporting unlawful behavior

Employees who are prepared to report corruption and discriminatory behavior are exercising initiative and this, if done appropriately, is generally considered reasonable grounds for exercising initiative.

Crisis management

During a crisis, it is appreciated and encouraged when employees exercise prudent initiative, as these predicaments are usually unique and without precedent.

With regard to the New Employment Relationship Model in Chapter 4, the individual parallel response to the value of open information is to be willing to contribute to the organizational decision-making processes. To display this mindset, individuals need to be willing to align their personal goals with those of the organization. In addition, individuals should make every effort to understand the parameters of, and be willing to exercise, enterprising behavior. Also, they should be prepared to understand their manager's point of reference, and be ready to accept their responsibility in being involved in the decision-making processes. To be able to do this, the organization needs to provide employees with access to information about organizational goals, needs, and HR systems. Specifically, this means putting in place strategies to align individual and organizational goals: defining, communicating, and encouraging appropriate enterprising behavior; sharing useful information; and discouraging initiative in certain areas by making the employee accountable for improper enterprise. These elements and the appropriate responses from both entities in the employment relationship will go a long way to shifting from a value of closed information to a value of open information.

The **10** Key Points …

1. Employers ought to be prepared to share information with their employees to enable them to be more enterprising.

2. The importance of open communication; the commercial advantages; the relevance of participation in decision making; and the fact that employees want a greater degree of autonomy are reasons for its inclusion in the New Employment Relationship Model.

3. The line between employee initiative and managerial responsibility is referred to as the "initiative paradox." The initiative paradox is defined as managing the extent and limits of employee participation in decision making.

4. There are four practical strategies help to overcome the initiative paradox. These are goal alignment, boundary refinement, information sharing, and active accountability.

5. Goal alignment is about aligning the perspectives of staff and management.

6. Boundary refinement involves a manager carefully communicating the kind of initiatives s/he wants and doesn't want.

7. Information sharing between employee and employer can build trust.

8. Active accountability involves an understanding between managers and staff that initiative and judgment can be exercised, but only at the employee's own risk.

9. The four strategies place limits on undesirable forms of initiative and at the same time encourage initiative in appropriate ways. The common factor in using all these strategies is open communication between employees and managers.

10. Well-managed firms use a combination of techniques to address the initiative paradox.

chapter 13

The Corporate Culture Change Cycle

Case Study

The traditional top-down approach to managing change that avoids the changing psychological contract is likely to continue to be flawed in bringing about transformation in the workplace.

In this final chapter I will use a case study to illustrate how the New Employment Relationship Model can be applied in an organization. The Lockyer Valley Regional Council, in its quest to become an employer of choice, has developed some practical strategies to alter the psychological contract. To achieve this, the organization used the Corporate Culture Change Cycle (CCCC). This will be discussed in this chapter.

Before we look at this methodology, let's recap the eight binding values of the New Employment Relationship Model. There are many overlaps between the eight values. If any value is neglected, it will undoubtedly adversely affect other values in the model. On the other hand, applying one or more values in an organizational setting will contribute to the development of other values. For instance, the value of flexible deployment is closely associated with the values of learning and development and open information. Developing a flexibly deployed workforce through the implementation of a successful multi-skilling program requires an emphasis on learning and development and the need for information sharing. All eight values are in some way interrelated.

The New Employment Relationship Model offers a comprehensive roadmap to navigate the transformation from a traditional to new employment relationship in an organization. A new psychological contract is the cornerstone of becoming an employer of choice. With more than two hundred years of conditioning, the challenges of changing the mindsets supporting the traditional employment relationship should not be underrated. Nonetheless, I have argued throughout this book that there is a need to alter these traditional mindsets. The costs to both the organization and individual are too great to continue with the "them and us" employment relationship mentality.

Attracting and Retaining Talent has given managers and management researchers a research-based model of a new psychological contract which is the type of workplace culture to become an employer of choice. I would like to suggest that the framework put forward in this book is a credible substitute for many outdated HRD strategies. These traditional HRD approaches often fail to take into account the revolution that has occurred in individual and organizational paradigms over the past thirty years. The traditional top-down approach to managing change that avoids the changing psychological contract is likely to continue to be flawed in bringing about transformation in the workplace.

What is the Corporate Culture Change Cycle?

The eight-step CCCC is a vehicle for transforming the culture of an organization, with respect to the employment relationship. The process begins by surveying the entire

The eight-step CCCC is a vehicle for transforming the culture of an organization

workforce. Its purpose is to gather data about the perceptions of organizational members on the elements of the eight values of the model. Once the results have been collected, they are analyzed from three organizational perspectives: Top Management (TopMgt), Middle Management (MidMgt), and Workforce (Work). Through this stratification, a comparative analysis between the three perspectives is undertaken, using a 360° instrument, which analyzes the extent of agreement or disagreement between the three organizational perspectives. From the eighty items in the survey, sixteen elements are then prioritized for further investigation by an ongoing project team. This project team is a representative slice of the organization. Practical recommendations are then made on the

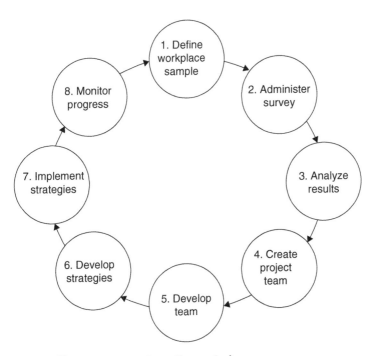

FIG 13.1 **The Corporate Culture Change Cycle**

This figure originated from www.winnersatwork.com.au/organisation.

team's consideration of the multisource perspectives in the survey analysis. As distinct from the traditional top-down method, the CCCC is based upon a bottom-up approach to change. The success of this approach is measured cyclically.

Figure 13.1 shows the eight steps in the cycle.

I will now briefly outline these eight steps, referring to the Lockyer Valley Regional Council.[1]

What is the Lockyer Valley Regional Council?

The Lockyer Valley Regional Council (LVRC) is a local government organization covering an area in the West Moreton region of southeast Queensland, Australia, between the cities of Ipswich and Toowoomba. It was created in 2008 during a merger of the Shire of Gatton and the Shire of Laidley. It has an estimated operating budget of A$35 million. The population in the region is approximately 30,000 residents. The Executive Leadership Team (TopMgt) consists of the chief executive officer and five directors. The LVRC is structured around five directorates: governance and performance; corporate and community services; planning and development services; infrastructure works and services; and organizational development and engagement. There are 402 staff in total.

The LVRC completed the CCCC in 2011 and 2013. The eight-step process is as follows.

Step 1: Define workplace sample

The workplace sample usually includes all staff. In 2011 and 2013, all staff at the LVRC were invited to participate in the survey by the CEO.

---

[1] For a fuller explanation of each step, refer to Chapter 13 of Baker T.B. (2009), *The 8 Values of Highly Productive Companies: Creating Wealth From a New Employment Relationship*. Brisbane: Australian Academic Press.

Step 2: Administer survey

The survey is administered online and can also be completed using paper and pencil. In the LVRC, the majority completed the survey online. For outdoor staff who do not normally have access to computers, the survey was completed using paper and pencil.

Participants were given a choice of three options for each of the eighty items (there are ten statements for each of the eight values): *agree, disagree,* or *neither agree nor disagree.* Provision for written comments was also available. For example, under the value of flexible deployment, one of the statements was: *I have a multi-skilling program in place in my team.* This was the statement that TopMgt and MidMgt responded to. Work answered the following statement: *My manager has a multi-skilling program in place for my team.* Essentially, this is the same question expressed differently to reflect the perspective of the person responding to it.

Step 3: Analyze results

An analysis of the survey results is then done across the three perspectives: TopMgt, MidMgt, and Work. TopMgt represents the organizational perspective, Work collectively represents the individual perspective, and MidMgt takes into account a third perspective.

In 2011, 71 percent of LVRC completed the survey and 58 percent in 2013.

Figures 13.2 and 13.3 show the aggregate results for both surveys for the LVRC.

In both figures, "D" stands for disagree, "P" for polarized,[2] "A" for agree, and "N" for neither agree nor disagree.

---

[2]"Polarized" refers to a result where there is an equal number of people agreeing and disagreeing.

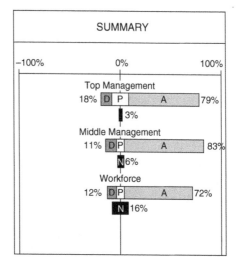

FIG 13.2 / **Aggregate survey results for 2011**

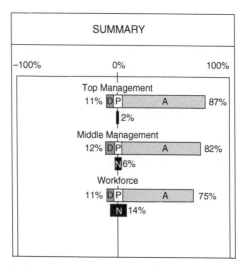

FIG 13.3 / **Aggregate survey results for 2013**

Step 4: Create project team

The composition of the project team is critical for its success. There is one essential criterion for selection. The condition is that the membership is as representative as possible of the entire organization.

In the LVRC, this consisted of two members of TopMgt, four members of MidMgt, and eight people representing Work. Within this project team of fourteen, there were representatives from each directorate.

Step 5: Develop team

As I pointed out in Chapter 8, it is important for the success of a newly-formed team to undergo some form of team development.

The project team at LVRC underwent a day of team development using the Team Management Profile methodology.[3] During this workshop we discussed the relative strengths and weaknesses of the team, based on the team's profile and ways to, respectively, maximize and minimize these characteristics.

Step 6: Develop strategies

After the successful completion of the team development workshop, the next focus for the project team is to tackle the sixteen-element agenda for change. In a structured process, the team reviews the qualitative results for each value and responds to the following two questions:

- What is the overall message for that value?
- What are two practical strategies for improving the survey results?

The result of this process is sixteen strategies for implementation.

---

[3] This was developed by TMS in Australia 25 years ago. You can find out more about TMS at www.tms.com.au.

For example, the LVRC project team reviewed the results for the value of customer focus in 2011 and summarized the results as follows:

- A need was identified for better two-way communication between departments (or what is commonly referred to as internal customer service), and
- A communication process to manage customer expectations.

As a result of these observations, the project team recommended the following two strategies:

- Develop a centralized process for recording information so that feedback can be given on successes as well as opportunities for improvement, and
- Establish an intranet to improve internal communications.

This information, along with the other strategies, was recorded in the report.

Step 7: Implement strategies

Once the report has been documented, the project team, in consultation with management, is in a position to implement strategies that aim to improve the perceptions from the survey results.

The LVRC project team decided to present a report to the executive team on their deliberations. Ninety-five percent of the recommendations made in 2011 have been successfully adopted and implemented.

Step 8: Monitor progress

The monitoring process should take place annually. This is done by repeating the cycle at the same time each year.

The LVRC elected to conduct the CCCC once every two years.

And that completes the process.[4]

In conclusion, the CCCC is a vital first step in an organization's move to becoming an employer of choice. The bottom-up approach to change I have just outlined relies heavily on the commitment of the cross-functional project team. The purpose of the cycle is to appraise how closely the individual and organizational entities are aligned to the New Employment Relationship Model (Chapter 4). This review is based on the aggregate perceptions of organizational members. A positive appraisal would suggest that elements of the eight values are evident within the current employment relationship. On the contrary, a lack of congruence would imply that elements of the model have yet to be embedded in the organizational culture. Irrespective of the outcome, the CCCC can provide a useful benchmarking mechanism for monitoring the psychological contract in an organizational setting. And, as I have argued throughout *Attracting and Retaining Talent*, a healthy employment relationship is the bedrock of becoming an employer of choice.

---

[4] If you would like more information on the CCCC, please visit www.winnersatwork. com.au.

Index

Printed and bound by CPI Group (UK) Ltd, Croydon, CR0 4YY